VIETNAM

ONE SOLDIER'S EXPERIENCE

By

Daniel H. Coughlin

authorHOUSE™

1663 LIBERTY DRIVE, SUITE 200
BLOOMINGTON, INDIANA 47403
(800) 839-8640
WWW.AUTHORHOUSE.COM

First published by AuthorHouse 11/14/07

ISBN: 1-4184-9101-2 (sc)
ISBN: 1-4184-9102-0 (dj)

Printed in the United States of America
Bloomington, Indiana

This book is printed on acid-free paper.

Library of Congress: 2007907945

Dedicated to the family, friends and loved ones of all who served in Vietnam.

Table of Contents

Introduction

I served with the 82nd Airborne, combat infantry, in Vietnam, from June 22, 1968 until July 2, 1969. There have been many perceptions about Vietnam, and the Vietnam Veteran but to date I have not come across anything that explains the Vietnam Experience.

Although it has been over twenty years since my return, I find more and more people asking me about Vietnam. It is difficult to discuss Vietnam with people who have not been there and it is something that I have avoided as much as possible. The usual questions that most people ask are: Did you see combat? Were you wounded? Did you ever kill anyone?

I was slightly wounded but never put in for a purple heart and I did kill, but by answering these questions you do not explain your combat experience. The only people who can identify with a combat veteran is another combat veteran, regardless of the war in which they fought. The only people who can really understand the Vietnam Combat Soldier is another Vietnam Combat Soldier. It makes no difference whether the person was wounded or if they ever killed anyone; if they were with a combat unit they can relate to the experience.

If this premise is true, that only one who experienced combat can understand combat, why am I writing this book? It's like having a toothache. If you ever had a serious toothache, you know the pain that you experienced. If you talk to someone who had one they can immediately relate to your situation but if you talk to someone who has never had a toothache they cannot really understand what you are going through. If someone wrote a detailed account of what it is like to have a toothache the non-tooth combatant will be better able to understand the situation, but without experiencing it they will never fully understand the pain. Like a woman who gives birth, as a man, I will never understand the pain or the joy that a woman experiences.

Through books, documentaries, and personal experience with childbearing women, I can come closer in my understanding of the experience but I will never really know what it is like to have a baby.

Through this book I hope to be able to take a person who is interested in the Vietnam experience and give them a fuller understanding of war, the Vietnam War and its effects on the Vietnam Veteran.

The 82nd Airborne was sent to Vietnam to help combat the Tet Offensive of 1968. The whole 82nd was not sent just one brigade. The 82nd was usually attached to units that needed our help at the time. In the course of my tour of duty, one year and ten days, we spent time working with Marines, Special Forces, the 101st Airborne, the 1st Calvary, the 9th Infantry, the 25th Infantry, the Vietnamese Regular Army and probably other units that do not come to mind at this time. We worked with some for as little as one operation and others for months at a time. The significance of working with so many different units is that you get to see a multi-faceted Vietnam.

The military broke Vietnam down into segments. There were four different areas of operations, II Core III Core, IV Core, and I Core. The reasoning for mentioning this is that the geography, and therefore the war itself, was vastly different, depending upon the area that you were in. I Core (Eye Corp) was at the northern end of South Vietnam. It started at the D.M.Z. and went south. In this area you basically had Marine and Airborne units. If you talk to someone from these units their experience will vary greatly from someone who spent their tour of duty in IV Core or the Mekong Delta area.

I spent my first four months in I Core. The geography there was mountainous. There was very thick foliage in places. You had what was called double or triple canopies that is trees that grow and overlap with each other where you could not see the sky.

They did not cover the whole area but were prevalent in many parts of I Core. This type of geography made it difficult to coordinate activities, supply could be a problem, at times you had to blast away trees in order to clear an L.Z. (Landing Zone for helicopters). Sometimes there was no place for an L.Z., food would run short, ammunition would run low, wounded would have to be carried in makeshift stretchers until they could be evacuated. Besides all this, you fought a different type of war up north. The main enemy that you encountered was the N.V.A. (North Vietnamese Army). These were disciplined, trained soldiers that worked as a regular army unit. When you engaged the enemy you fought a conventional type of war. Air support, in places, was non-existent because of the canopies, even artillery was a problem under these conditions.

In the southern parts of Vietnam the war was completely different. In the area north and west of Saigon the terrain was basically flat, consisting of rice paddies and low woodland areas. In the southernmost or delta region the land was basically flat but it was engulfed in a myriad of rivers, canals, streams and wetlands. In these areas supply or transportation was rarely a problem. The enemy you fought was also different. The V.C. or Vietcong were the main enemy of the area. The Vietcong were not a highly trained military unit as their counterpart in the north was, nonetheless they were a formidable enemy. They were, in general, a loose knit group of soldiers that engaged in guerilla type of tactics. They usually struck in small groups, relying on surprise, engaging us for only a few minutes, booby trapping their escape route, which made it difficult to pursue. Air support played a major role in this type of warfare.

The only region of Vietnam that I was never in was the central highlands. The soldiers who fought in that area probably had experiences that were unique in itself, but we all fought in what was known as the Vietnam War.

The Vietnam War is a difficult thing to explain. Aside from the peculiarities that arose in different geographical areas the war went on for over a decade. What I might have experienced in a particular area might be different from soldiers who fought years before or years after me.

I have decided not to do any research before writing this book. If some of the names of areas escape me or are not exactly correct, you will know the reason.

In the twenty odd years since returning I have never tried to dwell on or recall incidents that have taken place but some instances remain no matter what. Since deciding to write this book I have spent many sleepless nights, when you recall one instance another pops into your mind and your mind does not stop working. It is almost like turning on a VCR and reviewing the war. It seems as if it was only yesterday.

The thrust of this book is not to give a chronological account of the events that took place but rather deal with concepts or values and use various stories to help illustrate these concepts. All of the events that will be described in this book will be events that I personally experienced. The names of the people who served with me will be changed in order that certain incidents will not be used to embarrass anyone. Most people I served with were fine upstanding individuals and should be proud of their accomplishments.

Like the toothache, after a while you do not recall exactly how painful it really was, you just remember it was a painful experience.

Becoming A Soldier

In a few hours the plane will arrive in Vietnam. Just thinking about the prospect was frightening. The last words that my father said to me was, "Be a good soldier, but don't be a hero".

Be a good soldier. What does that mean?

Everything was happening so fast. A couple of months ago I was partying in Brooklyn and now I was about to become involved in a war. A war I was not even sure we should be fighting.

The one thing that I did know was that I was not going to die in Vietnam. I don't know how I knew this, I just knew. I guess dying was paramount in my mind.

"Fasten your seat belts, the smoking light is out, we are about to land at Bien Hoa airport."

As we departed the airplane there were people yelling, "Hurry up, double time to the bunkers!"

Looking around, there were sandbag tunnels everywhere. I had arrived in Vietnam.

Bien Hoa was like a personnel center for newly arrived and departing soldiers. For the newly arrived, it was typical army, hurry up and wait. For those going home you would think that it would be an exciting place, but most of the soldiers were almost expressionless. They would look at you as a new arrival and just say, "good luck." I asked one soldier what it's like out there. He started to tell me that you don't want to be out there. "You'd be lucky if you last a month."

His buddy then tapped him on the shoulder and said, "Come on, don't scare the kid. He'll find out soon enough."

As they walked away, they turned and said, "Good luck". The expression on their faces was sympathetic but horrifying enough to send chills down my spine.

The base itself was a fairly safe place. There were stories about rocket and motor attacks, but nothing happened during the few days that were spent there.

Each morning you would assemble in formation. They would call out names and the units that you were assigned to. The last thing you wanted to hear was your name called. Somehow you were hoping that they lost your paperwork.

Then one morning I heard, "Daniel Coughlin, one hundred and first airborne!"

101st Airborne! I was not airborne. The army had made a mistake and I was going to let them know about it!

After the call of the name I went to the sergeant in charge.

"There has been a mistake here. You assigned me to 101st, I am not airborne."

He said, "The army does not make mistakes. What is your name?"

He looked at the chart and looked at me, there was a smile on his face. "You're right soldier."

I knew it. Even the army could not make this much of a mistake. I never jumped out of a plane.

"You're assigned to 101st Airborne."

All my protesting meant nothing. There I was, flying up north to be a part of the 101st Airborne. I was later reassigned to the 82nd Airborne.

As it turned out, with the exception of the 173rd Airborne, which made two jumps in the early sixties, the airborne units were regular infantry. They did not jump out of planes. There were not enough regular airborne trained infantry to replace what was needed, so there I was a "Leg" being assigned to an airborne unit.

The first week up north was basically uneventful, more training, more Physical Training and the usual amount of menial tasks to be performed.

One evening after a training session, I was handed a sickle to cut the weeds that were growing in the compound. Not a bad assignment, much better than burning the shit, which was assigned the day before. As I aimlessly swung at weeds, I saw a snake. In a reflex action I swung the sickle and caught the snake right below the head and had it pinned to the ground. The snake was pinned, but alive and wiggling to get free. I looked around, there was no one in sight, so I kept the snake pinned to the ground. A few minutes later a sergeant came walking by. I yelled, "Hey sarge. I got a problem."

He walked up, looked at me, saw the situation, and said, "Don't let go."

He immediately put the heel of his boot on the snake's head, grabbing the tail of the snake with his hand, pulled hard, and separated the head from the rest of the body. He bent over and picked up the head of the snake by the back of the neck. "Let me show you something, private, this is a poisonous snake. You see the diamond shape of the head? Do you see those pockets protruding from the side? Well, that's where the poison is stored. You should learn to recognize a poisonous snake."

I thanked him and he began to walk away then turned around and said, "By the way, these usually travel in pairs. The other one will be back, looking for its mate."

It took me a second to realize what he had said, then I was gone before he took two more steps. Poisonous snakes! I haven't even been to the field yet. What's next?

We were about to board a helicopter to take us to the field. I was given an M79 grenade launcher as my weapon. The M79 was basically a simple weapon.

It opened in the middle like a shotgun, firing one grenade at a time. The grenades were different from the ones that you held in your hand. They were cylindrical, about five or six inches in circumference and about the same in length. All the ammunition, food, and water was carried in a ruck sack, which felt like it weighed about a hundred pounds and in fact it probably did.

We boarded the helicopter, I was sitting at the end. There were six of us in the chopper plus a pilot, co-pilot and two door gunners. As the chopper lifted off, I noticed that there were no doors, there was nothing between me and outside. I held on tight. The pilot turned around and said, "What do we have here, a bunch of cherries?" (New Recruits.) Then he proceeded to wave back and forth over the terrain. I tried to show no fear, I was not going to let him get the best of me, but you probably could not have pried my hands loose with a crow bar. Finally the chopper landed.

We got out in the middle of a field operation. "You go see the lieutenant, first platoon alpha company."

"Lieutenant, I am assigned to you."

"Sergeant Cody, this one's yours."

"What's your name?"

"Coughlin."

"Where do you come from?"

"Brooklyn."

"Where's that?"

"New York."

"Hey fellas, another New Yorker!"

After a bunch of disparaging remarks about New York, "Where did you go to jump school?"

"I didn't."

"Not another damn leg! This is an airborne unit!"

After being introduced to the people in my squad it was time to move. We had to climb a mountain in order to set up a N.D.P. (Night Defensive Position).

After one hour of climbing this mountain, we finally took a break. I thought, I'm never going to make it. The straps to my ruck sack felt like they were cutting through my shoulders. I felt physically exhausted. I wondered if everyone else was as tired as I was. By the time we took our second break, I was beyond tired, but at least I knew I wasn't alone, there was grumbling from everyone.

"All right, saddle up!"

Here we go again! The mountain looked straight up. You would follow the person in front of you and watch what they did. Grabbing a tree stump to pull you up or go twenty feet sideways to gain a few feet in height. About a half-hour out, I went to grab a tree stump, the support under my left foot gave way, my body turned sideways. The weight of my ruck sack pulled me backwards and I rolled five or six feet down the mountain. I landed on my back. Someone was calling for a medic.

"Are you all right?"

I shook my head yes.

"All right, take five. Are you sure you're all right?"

I felt like saying, no, I am not all right, I am damn exhausted, but I was more embarrassed than exhausted.

"I'm all right."

"Someone help him with his ruck sack. What do you have in this ruck sack? It weighs a ton!"

"Hey sarge, look at this! He's carrying enough ammo for the whole company. He must have over a hundred grenades, three claymores, and enough food for a month. Who packed this for you?"

"This is what they gave me at the rear, sarge."

"Those damn desk warriors! Lighten his load!"

As they began to distribute the ammo they should only know that it was I who packed all that ammo. I figured I was not going to the field without all the ammo I could carry. A rookie mistake. I was determined not to make another. It could cost me my life.

It took another couple of hours before we reached our destination. I was so, so tired, but I could not help to feel kind of good. I know everyone there was pulling for me. The support was exhilarating.

That night after we set up our perimeter, I was given fourth guard, it was time to sleep. There were no tents or sleeping bags or anything of that nature. You rolled up in something called a poncho liner and slept on the ground. I was asleep for what felt like about ten minutes when I was being awakened. I thought it can't be time for my guard already. It wasn't. The man in the position next to me was holding a piece of shrapnel. "This just landed between us."

"Are we being attacked?"

"No, I think it was from our own artillery."

"What can we do?"

"Nothing much."

So I went back to sleep.

The next couple of days were basically the same routine. You would get up before dawn. Hump the bush all day, set up your N.D.P or ambush and pull guard every two or three hours. Finally after three days our company was brought back to a fire base.

It was almost three months now since I landed in country. We had returned from a forty-three day mission. The usual length of a mission was to last anywhere from five to ten days but because of the circumstances they kept us in the field for forty-three straight days. We were at a base camp now, hot food, cold drinks, and a few new recruits.

One of the recruits was asking what it was like out there. How do you explain that to someone? In the past couple of months, I had been shot at, been under mortar attack, been shelled by our own artillery, seen men killed, carried wounded on makeshift stretchers, shot at the enemy, been in a fire fight, watched a helicopter crash, killing everyone on board, including the wounded that were being evacuated, been part of several combat assaults, was caught in a fire, captured enemy soldiers, overran an N.V.A base camp finding the largest cache of military weapons ever found in Vietnam at the time, watched our own Air Force bomb a mountain that was occupied by 101st Airborne, although we did not realize that at the time, and that's aside from other elements such as, the almost deafening sounds of a fire fight, the screaming of wounded, the dealing of chaotic situations in a controlled manner, fear, fatigue, and the natural surroundings that included land leeches that were so dense in spots that they could chase a whole army off of a mountain.

What's it like out there? It's hard to explain but I did know that somewhere along the line I had become a soldier.

Fear

In Vietnam you were at one level of fear or another the whole time you were there. There was a general level of fear that you experienced because of the fact that you were in a war zone. That fear was most intense during the first couple of months of duty. The intensity of that fear was actually a positive attribute. It made you alert and cautious and aware of your situation. After a couple of months the intensity of fear waned. This could cause you to become complacent and sloppy in your actions. You still experienced the fear but just at a mitigated level. Then your last couple of months the general level of fear became intensified. It was different from the fear you first experienced where the intensity was basically caused by the unknown. This intensity was caused by the realization that you were a short timer and going home was an attainable goal. It caused you to be nervous and become very conscientious about what was taking place.

Besides the general level of fear , which was always present, there were specific actions that raised the level to almost unbearable proportions.

The most intense fear that I have ever experienced came when I was in country about four weeks. We were on patrol when Charlie Company, about a half a click ahead of us, was ambushed. The fire fight was intense. You could hear the sounds of the enemy rifles, they were distinct. The order came down to drop ruck sacks and pursue. The closer we came to Charlie Company the less fire we heard. As we approached the area you could smell the gunpowder. The enemy was in retreat. The casualties were heavy. Our platoon was ordered to secure an L.Z so that we could medivac the wounded and remove the dead. The rest of the company pursued the enemy. The only sound of enemy gun fire you heard was sniper fire. The N.V.A used snipers very effectively in order to slow down the pursuit.

We were lucky there was a clearing large enough for a helicopter to land. The first sergeant of Charlie Company came to the L.Z. There was a bullet lodged in his helmet; you thought that only happened in Hollywood. The choppers came and the casualties were removed. The first sergeant said that they were hit by a company of N.V.A. regulars.

We regrouped, picked up our ruck sacks, Charlie Company headed in one direction. We pursued in another. My squad was the point squad, I was about seventh in line. We knew the enemy was out there. We moved slowly and cautiously. Things were very quiet. The terrain was rough, mountainous, with a thick underbrush. It was getting late, we knew we had to find an N.D.P. Then we came upon a trail that was wide enough and clear enough to drive a truck through. There was blood all over the trail. It was getting dark. We set up an N.D.P. on a hill overlooking the trail.

As I was setting the claymore out in front of our position I could feel the enemy out there. You knew that the trail was large enough to move a regiment through. We set up at one hundred percent alert.

As we lay at our positions we were anticipating an attack. Then there was a loud scream and moaning. We could hear movement. Sound travels far at night, but it seemed like it came from about a hundred yards in front of us. The orders were not to fire unless we saw the enemy. They did not want to give away our position. I thought, give away our position? They know exactly where we are. There were more screams. The N.V.A. must have been either treating or moving the wounded, the anticipation was mounting. Off and on the screaming continued. Artillery was being called in. We thought we saw movement in front of us. The officer who was calling in the artillery was about ten yards behind us.

We asked for illumination. There was definite movement about two hundred yards ahead of us, right where the trail was. The lieutenant called for high explosive rounds. The first round landed right in the center of our own N.D.P., about twenty yards behind me. The sound was almost deafening. You could feel the earth shake, and sounds of metal whizzing by. People were yelling for medics. The lieutenant called for a repeat round, one hundred yards down and one hundred yards left. The lieutenant was in country less time than I was. Luckily the R.T.O. (Radio Telephone Operator) was alert. He told the lieutenant not to call for a repeat round, that there was something wrong. He listened. People were scrambling everywhere. The medic could not handle all the wounded. People were helping. The R.T.O. called for a medivac. There was a burning on my wrist. Some of the aftermath of the explosion had landed on my wrist, it hurt but it wasn't that bad. I trained my eyes to look ahead. I knew among this havoc it would be an ideal time for the enemy to strike. Now I could hear yelling and screaming from inside the perimeter and periodic screaming and moaning from outside the perimeter. The medivac choppers arrived. They lit up the N.D.P. with their search light. It took two choppers to evacuate everyone. My heart was pumping, I could feel the blood rushing through my veins. Surely we would have to move our position. It was standard procedure after contact. No orders came down to move. The more you looked out the more everything seemed to move. My body felt like it was expanding. More screaming and moaning.

Come on, where are you? If you're going to attack, attack. I had never felt so scared in my life. My body started shaking. I was thinking, calm down, just be ready for them when they come. Where are they? Here they come, I can hear them. Why haven't the trip flares gone off? My mind would not stop working. I knew how scared I was. I felt all alone. It was up to me. Here they come. I know they're coming. Come on you bastards, you're not going to get by me.

My mind was going a mile a minute. The anticipation of being attacked was causing this acceleration. The anticipation was also causing an acceleration of fear, which by now had manifested itself within me. I was in a state of fear which just kept building. I knew that I had to control the fear but it was creating a physical sensation that there was something inside of me that was trying to get out. My body felt like it was about to burst. I physically had to do something in order to release this fear from within me but the only thing that I could do was lay there in anticipation of an enemy attack. With each passing minute I summoned up all discipline that I could muster to control what was taking place inside of me. I stayed in this state for about an hour.

Now there was nothing, no screaming, no moaning, no sound of movement. I started to calm down. It became apparent that if they were going to attack they should wait for dawn. We went on fifty percent alert, but I don't think anyone really slept.

Dawn came and the fear came back but it was much less than what I experienced the night before. Daylight came and there was no one out there. What a relief. There was a level of fear in me, but the intensity was gone.

That morning everyone was basically silent. My wrist was still burning. I showed it to the medic. He had a cold look in his eye.

"One of the guys had his balls blown off."

"How many were killed?"

"At least two, and some others pretty bad. Your wrist is okay. Use this salve to prevent any infection. I could put you in for a Purple Heart."

I just shook my head no. After what these guys suffered, who wanted a Purple Heart?

By the time we were ready to move out. I knew everyone was as scared as I had been, but we all came through it.

This was the most fear I had ever experienced, yet it was not the first time I had been involved in combat.

About ten days prior, we had encountered a couple of snipers. They called for grenade launchers up front. I was scared. There was a level of fear that ran through my body but nowhere near that intensity. It was probably because we were doing something. We were being fired at, but my team was pursuing. We spotted the sniper in a tree, we fired, he was history. The other sniper got away.

It seems that fear manifests itself most when there is nothing you can do about it and the longer that happens the more the fear builds.

We were heading out on ambush one night. I was in country seven or eight months at the time. We were working down south in the delta region. It was not a good area. We were leaving from a fire base. They had flack jackets there. It was the only time that I had ever worn one. Some guys took them, some didn't.

We set up our ambush in a dry rice paddy. A rice paddy was a small area of land, roughly twenty to thirty yards square that was surrounded by dikes that were raised a few feet above the ground. In the wet season the dikes would contain water. In the dry season, the bed was as hard as concrete. There was usually a multitude of rice paddies in a field. The rice paddy was only a few hundred yards from a village. We set up around the perimeter. I was sleeping when a loud explosion rang out. An R.P.G. landed in the perimeter. The people on guard were yelling, incoming. I grabbed my weapon, ammo, and helmet, flack jacket and crawled next to the dike. Another rocket hit the perimeter. I pulled the flack jacket over me. In one hand I had my weapon. The other was protecting my balls. The only part of me that was exposed was the lower part of my legs. Another round hit. The fear was building.

What if they decide to attack? I'm just lying here. Don't stick your head out. BOOM!!! Another rocket. I could hear someone yelling, "I'm hit, I'm hit!" About thirty seconds went by. It's over. I began to raise my head to look around the area. BOOM!!! I saw an explosion. My head was down before the noise hit my ears. My adrenaline was flowing, my heart was beating heavily. A million thoughts were racing through my mind. I knew this feeling. Thirty seconds went by, there was silence. I raised my head.

"Is everyone all right?"

"I need a medic."

"Where did it come from?"

"I saw a flash about 200 yards ahead. Machine guns. Seventy niners over here."

We started firing into the area. All of a sudden the intensity of fear was gone. A couple of minutes later a medivac came along with a gun ship that we used to call Snoopy. It was not a helicopter, but a single or double engine plane. It could cause havoc.

There were only two wounded, both with "million dollar wounds," that is serious enough to send them to the hospital but no real damage done. As the medivac lifted out Snoopy continued to rain bullets on the area. We moved out in the dark of night to set up a new position.

Although the level of fear in me was high, especially moving at night, the intensity that I had built up while I was lying there helpless was gone. It seems that as soon as you react to a situation you vent a certain aspect of your fear. There were numerous other times when I was under attack and scared, but I'll use just one other example to illustrate a point.

Again we were in a bad area and this was the only time that we dug foxholes during my tour. I had just completed digging the foxhole and was going out to set a claymore mine. The artillery was prepping the area in front of us. There were explosions going off constantly. I was lying in a prone position setting my claymore when a mortar round exploded around ten feet in front of me. Luckily I was in a prone position and the thrust of the explosion went over me. You could tell by the sound that it was enemy mortar fire and not our artillery. It took me about a second to react and I was headed for the foxhole, yelling, "Incoming! Incoming!" As I lay in the foxhole, mortar fire was going off everywhere. It lasted about five minutes. During that time, I just laid in the foxhole, hoping I wouldn't take a direct hit. The adrenaline started pumping as soon as I jumped in the hole but the intensity of fear that was in me was not that great. Although the situation was grave, the anxiety was not building. Perhaps because I did not feel any real danger of being attacked once the mortaring stopped. Don't get me wrong. I was scared, but I was not experiencing the high level of fear that I had in other situations. Perhaps the foxhole gave me a feeling of security or I knew my reactions to fear.

Just what is fear? I know that there are different types of fear and varying level of fear, but I am not really sure that I can define exactly what fear is. I know it is something that is real and is a definite reaction to a dangerous or potentially dangerous situation. Is there a levels of fear which we should consider normal for a particular situation? What part does the mind play in mitigating or over development of such fears?

We were working in the delta region when we came upon an old French outpost that was overlooking a river. The river was narrow and very turbulent at this point. They had built a footbridge across the river. The bridge consisted of a flank of wood about two inches wide, twenty-five feet long and about six inches deep. We used this footbridge to cross the river.

I have never really been in love with heights. No phobia, but I just don't like them. I was the third person to go across the bridge. To me it was like walking a tightrope. I slowly started to walk across, taking each step carefully. I got about ten feet out when the bridge started to sway. An instant level of fear came upon me, equal to anything that I had experienced. My body started shaking, I did not want to take the next step. My shaking caused the bridge to sway more. There I was with a sixty pound ruck sack on my back, a weapon in my hands, about twenty feet over a river, that if I fell, there was probably no way I would survive. They say not to look down, but that was impossible, you had to look where you were walking. I took another step, I was shaking even more. It felt like I was losing my balance. My heart was in my mouth. Another step, then another. My body was still shaking, the fear was immense. Somehow I made it across. When I got across, I breathed a sign of relief and the fear was gone. Most of the others crossing the bridge straddled it, putting one leg on each side, inching their way across. I wish I had thought of that.

A few days later, on the return trip, there was that bridge again. I walked across it with no problems. There was a fear, but little in comparison. Why?

Because I dealt with the fear in the appropriate manner which in essence created a change in me. The change was simply the fact that I knew that this fear would not control me.

The fear I experienced crossing the bridge was intense and life threatening but different from combat situations probably because I was the one in control of the situation, rather then the situation being in control of me.

There are all types of fear and people react in varying ways. There is nothing wrong with fear. It's how you react to the fear that will make you or break you.

There was a cherry who came out to the field when I was in country about six or seven months. The first night he pulled guard he started shooting up the place.

"What happened?"

"I saw movement out there."

We had to move our night position. Nobody liked moving at night. His second guard that same night, the same thing. We talked to him. Explained that if you stare at something long enough at night everything will look like it is moving. The next night we gave him a starlight scope, a device that enables you to see at night. No matter, the same thing, he started shooting at everything. There we were, we had to move again. We didn't let him pull guard again that night. The next night he was on ambush, we did not let him pull guard by himself. It didn't matter, he started shooting up the place, but this time, he came running back towards my position. He's lucky we did not blow him away. We took his weapon from him. The next day he was out on the field.

He let his fear get the better of him. Rather than controlling it he had to vent it because he let it control him. He's lucky he was not killed because of his actions.

Fear shows itself in many ways. I remember when I first started to get to know some of the guys in my platoon. We were at a base camp and the guy was telling a story about walking point one day. "There I was traipsing through the jungle and I came upon the point man for the N.V.A. We startled each other. The son of a bitch ran one way and I ran the other."

The way he told the story, everyone laughed, but I couldn't help wonder why he just did not shoot him. Now about seven months later, the same guy was a sergeant and was pulling ambush one night. He was out on a squad size ambush, about eight or nine men, with another sergeant, an instant N.C.O., that is, someone who trained ninety days back in the States and became a sergeant. He was in country less than two months.

They had set up to ambush a trail. The instant N.C.O. was on guard in one position, and the sergeant at the other. The instant N.C.O. was the first to spot the V.C. There were about twenty of them carrying rockets, machine guns, and were heavily armed. He alerted the sergeant and the rest of the men. The V.C. walked right into the kill zone, set for ambush. They both decided not to fire. They did not even alert other ambushes set in other areas that there was movement.

The next day when we all regrouped, the story came out. I asked the sergeant what happened.

"Did you have your claymore set?"

"Yes."

"Did they walk in your kill zone?"

"Yes."

"Well, what happened?"

"There were too many of them. I was afraid they would overrun our position."

"Are you crazy? With that type of an ambush set you could blow your claymores, throw grenades, use your seventy niners, and the machine gun would take care of anything that might be left." I shook my head in disgust and walked away.

Most soldiers would love to be in a position to spring that type of ambush.

The grumbling among the troops was intense. Everyone was pissed. A group came up to me, probably because they thought I was fair, and asked what I thought about the situation. I thought for a second, but there was really no need. I said, "it sucks." What happens tomorrow or the next day if we get blown away by this group of V.C.? How many of us might die or get maimed because they were to afraid to act?. If even one of us gets hurt, I think they should be shot. I know this sounds a little strong, but, fuck them!"

Most agreed. A couple looked at me in amazement, I think they were expecting something a little softer.

I looked over at the two sergeants, who were sitting isolated by themselves. They looked like two scared kids who just had their hands caught in the cookie jar, it was a pathetic sight. They were both taken out of the field. I do not know what happened to them.

Fear is based on three things. First is the situation that you are in, second is the degree of anticipation caused by the situation, and third is your reaction to the situation and anticipation.

How fear affects you is a very subjective and individual thing.

Franklin Delano Roosevelt stated that "there is nothing to fear except fear itself." He was simply stating that the situation that you are in does not call for fear. Therefore the anticipation that was being created and the reaction to the anticipation is unfounded.

In Vietnam by the mere presence of you being there was cause for fearful situation. The fact that you were on combat duty heightened the situation and the fact that you were in combat brought the situation to another level but the situation is not always in direct proportion to the fear that is being experienced.

Take the sniper attack. This was a very real and dangerous situation, bullets were being fired directly me, yet there was no time for anticipation because of the immediate reaction to the situation. Fear existed but did not have time to manifest itself. You tend to transcend the fear and react to the situation.

The time that we set up the N.D.P. overlooking the trail and got hit by our own artillery, the enemy never really fired at us yet the fear just kept building. There was no reaction to the situation so the anticipation just kept mounting. In retrospect, the enemy was not going to attack. They were looking to get the hell out of there but at the time, the anticipation of their attack created a fear in me that is really indescribable. If they had attacked we could have reacted and the fear would not have manifested itself as had happened in R.P.G. rocket attack.

Everyone understood the fear in the cherry who fired at nothing. We all at one time or another pulled guard when anticipation of attack was almost overwhelming but you had to learn to control your anticipation and not to react to an unwarranted situation.

The fear that is actually created in one's own mind is probably the most devastating fear of all for it is in no way related to the reality of the situation and therefore could eat away at your confidence and your ability to react in a proper manner.

The case of the two sergeants borders on cowardice. They chose not to react to a real situation. You might think that their fear of being overrun was warranted, but believe me, in a properly executed ambush they would face little if any danger. They allowed their fear to create an error in judgment that they tried to rationalize as being acceptable. If you could have seen the look on their faces you would know, that they knew that they had screwed up. I wonder how much that has affected them in later life.

For that matter, what residual effect has fear played in all of our lives? As I was writing this chapter I could feel a level of anxiety flowing through me. Tears would come to my eyes for no apparent reason. It was not like I was thinking of people who were being killed or wounded, then I could understand the tears. I know recalling these experiences is not good for my mental well being. The tears are probably a transference of emotions. While I was experiencing the fear I never cried but while I'm recalling it, my emotions have become heightened. I guess the tears are just a release.

I thought that I had adjusted well, but now I'm not sure how the whole damned experience had affected me. I do know, however, that because of my experience with fear and my ability to deal with it in a proper manner it has made me a stronger person.

Morals

Everyone came to Vietnam with the same Christian/Judeo moral concepts. Among the most highly regarded of these concepts is the commandment "Thou shalt not kill."

I don't think anyone who first came to Vietnam envisioned themselves as a killer. Although we were trained to kill, had instilled in us that it was our job to kill, and during training had killing constantly reinforced in our mind, most of us did not think of ourselves as killers. In fact I am sure everyone was wondering what it would be like to have to kill somebody and if the time came could they do it?

Soon after arriving in country most of the moral questions that you brought with you evaporated. You had one basic goal and that was to stay alive. Stay alive by any means possible. It was either you or them, everything else was irrelevant. You did not care whether the war was right or wrong or what commandment you happened to be infringing upon. You just wanted to survive.

The first sniper attack that I was involved in, there were at least four of us shooting at the sniper. I remember looking at the dead body on the ground. This was first dead person that I had ever seen outside of a funeral parlor. The absence of life was a little chilling.

Who got him? Did you get him? No one was really sure. A sergeant came over to retrieve his rifle.

"Come on let's go, don't bunch up."

He must have overheard our conversation. He said, "it doesn't matter who killed him, we all killed him."

Walking away, I thought this was a little strange, the sergeant wasn't even shooting at him.

After that most of the fire fights, and there really weren't that many, unless you were involved in the initial contact you really weren't sure who killed whom. Once you started firing there would be so much fire power all going basically in the same direction that it was impossible to keep a score card. Believe it or not this became frustrating. You knew the enemy was out to kill you and your job as a soldier was to kill the enemy. You got to the point that you wanted to kill. You wanted to know that you were the one that killed the enemy.

It was Christmas Eve and I guess most of the people in the world (term used for the United States) were feeling good because our boys in Vietnam had a cease fire. This was only public relations. With the exception of one person from each company who was sent to the rear to see Bob Hope, it was business as usual. It had to be that way. How could you take time out from a war, let your enemy move supplies and ammunition, gain vantage points, then continue three days later.

The whole concept was ludicrous.

That night we set up a squad size ambush overlooking a river. I was on guard and could hardly believe my eyes. There was a sanpan coming down the river, then there were two and yet another. I alerted everyone in our position and the other ambush a little ways down the river. There they were V.C. moving supplies. We were about to trigger an ambush. My adrenaline started pumping. I set my sights on the guy standing in front on the first boat, waited till they were directly in front of us about twenty-five yards away. I squeezed the trigger of my seventy-nine. BOOM!! A direct hit. Then everyone opened up. It was like a turkey shoot. They returned some minimal fire but to no avail. We wreaked havoc on them. I finally stopped firing because I only had about ten grenades left. Eventually the gun ships came but there was no one alive by then.

The feeling that came over me was exhilarating. I was almost in the state of ecstasy. My first confirmed kill. There are at least eight or nine other V.C. and I probably killed more than one, but who could tell? I knew that I got the first one. It was a feeling that I never will forget.

There were other times we had the enemy in similar situations but each incident has its own reality.

We were out on a company sized patrol when we stopped along the bank of a river to eat. I heard some talking and laughing, there was brush in front of me and I could not see anything, I looked at my partner.

"Did you hear anything?"

"Yeah, I heard my stomach growling, I'm hungry."

There it was again, this time he heard it. We passed the word along. Next thing, "M79ers up front." I low crawled about twenty yards. "Hold your positions." All these commands were passed in a whisper soldier to soldier. I stopped, raised my head, and through a small opening in the brush I saw that across the river about seventy-five yards away were six or seven V.C. washing their clothes and playing in the river. I thought it was incredible that they did not hear us. You cannot imagine the noise a company size patrol can make especially when we were stopping to eat. Then the word, "get ready to fire." The seventy-nine, about twenty feet to my left opened up first. He hit a tree directly behind two of them. I fired, everyone started firing. I think I got a hit. There was return fire from the brush on the other bank. I only fired about five more rounds. The V.C. were either hit or gone before I fired my third round. This time there was no real thrill, no feeling of ecstasy. There was an excitement that ran through me but I was more concerned about staying alive then killing.

The principle of doing anything you can to stay alive replaced most moral precepts.

We were on patrol approaching a village that was not in a safe area. As we entered the village we saw the same basic inhabitants as in most isolated villages, small children, pregnant women, and a few older mamasons and papasons. There was never a male above the age of thirteen, they were either in one army or another.

You knew that when you saw pregnant women that they probably became this way because their V.C. husbands had been around. You started to equate pregnant women to a nonfriendly village.

We were about half way through the village, checking each hut for contraband when there was an explosion. Someone had tripped the booby trap. Everyone was frozen in their tracks. The order came down to grab a couple of the kids. At first I thought that was strange. Then came "point squad, put your weapons to their heads and have them walk you out of here. We will wait for the medivac. If they walk you through any booby traps blow their heads off." You could see the look of terror in the kids. I didn't know how to feel about the situation. My first reaction was that these were just kids and we were acting like bullies, but that was wrong. In reality these kids knew exactly where any booby traps might have been placed. The kids walked us through the village to a point about one hundred yards outside. There we stopped to wait for the others. The medivac came and the wounded were removed. Then the order came, "burn down the village." Two squads systematically went from hut to hut, each had a kid with a rifle to their head, and set them afire. When everyone was clear of the village we let the kids go. When we got a few hundred yards form the village you could hear explosions.

Now I could just hear the moralists having a ball with these scenarios. How could you burn down a village occupied by innocent women, old men and children? How could you use innocent children as pawns in your combat action? These are immoral acts and should be dealt with accordingly.

Well, that's easy for them to say sitting in their ivory towers but let me tell you the reality of the situation. These actions became standard operating procedures. If we came upon a village that we might even suspect of being hostile, we would grab the first kids that we could find, put a rifle to their heads, have them walk us from hut to hut, and eventually out of the village.

The end result of these procedures was that we never set off another booby trap while in a village and therefore never had to burn down another village. No physical damage ever came to one of these kids, but had they walked us into a booby trap or an ambush their heads would have been splattered all over that village. The V.C. knew this, they knew we meant business.

The moralists might say that this may be so but the ends never justify the means.

Well again this is easy to say sitting in your ivory tower but let it be them whose life is on the line and their philosophy will change. It would boil down to the least common denominator. It is either us or them and if you did not adhere to that you would probably be dead.

We were on patrol one day when we were hit by an ambush. The attack lasted about two minutes. We had with us a medic who entered the army as a conscientious objector. This man was no coward, at the time of his induction I am sure that he truly believed that his status as a C.O. was morally correct. After a few months in the field he started to carry a rifle.

This particular day when we were ambushed somehow none of us were hit. We returned fire and obtained the superior fire that is essential in this type of situation. The enemy stopped firing. We went in pursuit. We moved cautiously always mindful that the escape route could either be booby trapped or a sniper was left behind. We went over this small hill and in the ravine about ten yards in front of us lay a V.C. half dead with a rifle in his hand. He made a slight move. There was rifle fire. Almost before the rest of us reacted the V.C. lay there dead with about another ten bullets in him. I looked to my left and there was the medic, he just ended this man's life.

"He was going to shoot us."

Now I am not sure if that was the exact situation but with the rifle in his hand, if not the medic, someone else would have shot him.

A moralist would have said that medic had violated his principles but like the rest of us the moral principles that you thought were so pronounced while you were stateside soon changed to the simple concept: either us or them. The rest became superfluous.

By no means am I trying to say that because you're in a combat situation that life became cheap or that everyone had the attitude that it means nothing to kill. On the contrary, life becomes very precious, especially for those that you were with, and killing was part of staying alive. However there were instances when people's judgment became erratic.

We were in the rear guarding a bridge, which was basically good duty. There were Vietnamese soldiers that were permanently assigned to guard this bridge. Across from the bridge there was a house of ill repute. The women were allowed to be there during the day but were supposed to leave at night. For the American soldier it was somewhat of a rest, most partaking of the services offered by these women.

About an hour before dusk the women were made to leave the area, but supposedly unknown to the brass, the women would "sneak" back into the area at night through a hole in the fence. Everyone knew what was going on and most of us were happy for this breach in policy. One soldier, in my squad, was very upset over the fact that the girls would come back into the area.

"How do we know that they are not V.C. coming back at night?"

We told him that these ladies were checked out by the South Vietnamese before entering but this didn't seem to influence him.

"I don't care who checks them out. They should not be here and if they try to come through the fence tonight I am going to blow them away."

"Don't be crazy. These girls are here for us to have a good time. They are not V.C. They're whores. You know that and we know that."

"I don't care. They're not supposed to be here."

Nothing much more was said.

Come nightfall we noticed the soldier in question missing. A couple of us went over to the fence and there he was setting ambush on the area. The girls started to come. We stopped him from firing.

"What's wrong with you guys? I could have lit them up and I would have been right. They're not supposed to be here. I'm going to tell the captain."

I was never really sure if he just wanted to kill them because he knew that he would get away with it or somewhere in his mind he rationalized that killing them was the right thing to do. I am just glad that we stopped him from what I would have considered to be murder.

Sometimes there are circumstances that can take a situation that might appear black and white and put it into a cloudy area.

One day we were on road security, that is, we were flanked on either side of the road to make sure a truck convoy would not be ambushed. It was basically good duty. There was only one prior time in the eight or ten times that we pulled this duty that there was ever any trouble. That was about eight months prior, up north, when we got mortared.

This day we had a new man with us. He wasn't a cherry. He had been in country about as long as I had been but he was a truck driver. They sent him out to the field about a week prior because of some problems he was having. This was unusual. Usually it was the other way around. The problem people would be sent to the rear. I think they wanted to teach him a lesson.

He was assigned to my platoon, I knew him slightly when he was in the rear and got to know him a little better since he was in the field.

That day should have been routine. The engineers would sweep the road for mines, the convoy would pass and we would go pull an ambush somewhere.

The new guy was about thirty yards down the road from me. The convoy was just starting to pass when, BOOM! There was a big explosion. The second or third truck in had hit a land mine. The truck was blown off the road. Both the passenger and the driver were killed. The new guy went down to the road to see what had happened. He knew both of the occupants. There were four kids about ten yards from the explosions. They seemed to be laughing. He locked and loaded his sixteen and blew the four of them away.

He said that they were laughing at his friends who had just been killed and they were probably the ones who set the mine.

The mothers of the children came and started crying. They were escorted from the area. The guy who shot the kids was taken into the rear.

The whole episode was a big mess. The engineers, who usually were very good, somehow missed this mine. The new guy, who never should have been out in the field to begin with, apparently had just snapped. The kids who should have been confined to their village must have come to see what the explosion was about. The mothers whose kids lay dead on the ground were dragged away screaming and hollering.

The end result was two Americans and four Vietnamese kids were dead and the new guy was back out into the field two days later without even a reprimand.

Was this guy wrong in shooting these kids? I am sure that their mothers thought so. The army, on the other hand, either believed his explanation or did not want to deal with the situation.

From my point of view it is a tough call. My initial reaction was that he never should have done it, but who knows? Here is a guy, new to the field, involved in his first semi-combat situation, was probably very scared and then faced the following: the explosion happened right in front of him. He went to help and saw two of his long time buddies sitting there dead. He turned around and there was a group of kids laughing. Who knows what went through his mind? He might have equated these kids to the killer of his buddies. He blew them away and at the time felt justified in doing so.

He was wrong but I was glad to see that nothing happened to him for his apparent error in judgment.

What about the dead kids? There was a war going on, while they might have been just innocent bystanders, the people in the village were not. The V.C. did not operate in a vacuum. They knew exactly what the V.C. had done and probably helped them do it.

While it was not bad enough that our moral values were skewed, the military and political leaders made their own rules from the Geneva convention to regulating where one was or was not allowed to fire their weapon.

In Vietnam they made up arbitrary boundaries for free-fire zones or non-fire zones. I was never really sure what they were supposed to mean. I suppose in a free-fire zone you are allowed to shoot anyone in the area and in a non-fire zone you could only shoot if you were fired at. I do not think anybody paid it too much attention.

We were up north and it was my first time walking point. The point man was simply the first man in the column. We were in a hostile area which by the rules was classified a free fire zone.

I remember being a little nervous. It was the first time that the point was my responsibility. There were people saying that I should not be walking point. It was not the job of someone carrying an M79. It belonged to a rifleman. Nonetheless there I was. We were in a mountainous region but the path we took was a fairly level plane crossing the top of the mountain. There were supposed to be no civilians in the area.

We were about half a click out when I spotted movement. This was not my first combat situation. I fell to the ground, alerted my slack man, aimed my 79 but noticed it was an old man standing in front of a hut. I was about to fire anyway but it just did not seem like a threatening situation.

"Pass the word back that we have a village up here."

We advanced and there was a small village, women, children, and old people. We searched the village, it was clean.

"Lieutenant, what's going on here, I thought there was not supposed to be any civilians in the area.

He really did not have a worthwhile response. If I had fired like I was supposed to in this situation there would have been a lot of innocent people killed and the army probably would have given me a medal for it. What a war!

The Geneva Convention was another seeming paradox. Rules for war. I am sure that they are necessary but I don't think that any field soldier knew exactly what they were. We heard tracer bullets and white phosphorous rounds were outlawed because of their burning affect. Yet every machine gun had a tracer bullet every fourth round and white phosphorous grenades were issued to the seventy niners.

The rules governing prisoners of war probably made some sense but the American army bypassed them in a way. We did not interrogate the POW's, we turned them over to the South Vietnamese Army.

One day on a routine patrol we came across a Vietnamese male in his twenties. Any male in his teens or older was automatically taken as a prisoner. They might not necessarily be the enemy but we took them in as a matter of procedure, at least in most areas. This particular day we were based in a village, we returned there with the prisoner. We turned the prisoner over to our lieutenant who in turn called the South Vietnamese to relinquish the prisoner to them. Normally the Vietnamese would take the prisoner back to a prison compound and interrogate them there. This day the Vietnamese did not do that. They took the prisoner into one of the huts in the village and interrogated him there. After a few minutes there was some loud shouting and then a blood-curdling scream. We could not see what was going on but we knew that they were torturing him. Then some more screams.

"Lieutenant, put a stop to this."

Others were saying, leave them alone, he's probably a V.C. anyway. Then some more screams.

"Lieutenant, put a stop to this or we are going to."

"Okay."

The lieutenant went into the hut. He came out a few minutes later and tried to explain that there was nothing he could do about it. Once we turn a prisoner over to the Vietnamese he is under their authority and the U.S. Army had no jurisdiction. Another scream. We got our weapons and we headed towards the hut. The lieutenant stopped us and started talking to us. He could have ordered us out of there but I am not sure that we would have listened. Then from out of the hut emerged the two Vietnamese officers. They got their jeep and drove away. One of the guys looked into the hut. The prisoner was dead. We never even knew whether he was a V.C. or not. Now he was just dead. As far as the U.S. Army was concerned they did nothing to violate the Geneva Accord; after all it was out of their jurisdiction.

The third squad had sprung an ambush one night. They were moving back towards our position. One of the southerners came back, looked at me and said, "I got him. He walked right into my path and I blew him away." There was an excitement, he had a glow about him, I knew what he was feeling.

Then when everyone had returned the order came down to sweep the area. A standard procedure. This was something we all hated to do. We had to go out in the darkness and cover the area where the contact had been initiated. For what reason we did this, I was never really sure. That night as we were sweeping the area we encountered gun fire. It appeared to have come from one of three huts that sat isolated in the middle of nowhere. We returned heavy fire at the huts. Someone yelled, "Set them on fire." The machine guns started firing tracers at the grass roofs. The seventy niners fired white phosphorous rounds, all three hooches were in flames. We continued firing until we were satisfied that nothing could be alive. Because of the flames we did not approach the huts, we set up in another position a few hundred yards away. The next day one of the squads went back to the area. There were no V.C. found, just dead women and children in the huts.

Should this situation have caused a moral dilemma? We had just killed women and children. We used ammo that was supposedly banned by the Geneva convention. Nobody cared. I do not think that anyone even really thought about it. You see these moral concepts were not part of us. We had a very simple moral philosophy during combat situations. It was either kill or be killed. Thou shalt not kill was something that was left behind in Sunday schools back in the world.

You would probably think that religion and God would play a large part in the life of a combat soldier. They did not. They were rarely ever spoken of. I am not saying that they did not exist in people's minds but if they did it became a very personal thing.

People knew what they had to do to stay alive and I do not think they put much credence in God or religion doing that for them. They say that there are no atheists in foxholes. That may be true but religion was not a major factor, you relied on yourself and your ability to react to the situation to keep you alive. Especially the more you experienced combat.

One instance while we were being mortared one person was yelling, "Go ahead God, kill me. I dare you to kill me!" He was yelling these things till the attack stopped. Then he yelled, "Fuck you God, I'm still here!"

While most of us probably thought that this guy was pushing his luck, we also knew that God or religion had nothing to do with our survival.

Most veterans reading this now will probably say that what I am saying here is not true. All I can say is do not remember things from your new moral precepts that you adhere to now. We all had to reevaluate our moral values when we returned. Remember who you relied on to stay alive. Did you really rely on God to bring you through or did you rely on yourself and the people who were with you?

In combat situations moral values only existed to the point of your own survival and that of the people that you were with. Do you think any of us were bothered by initiating an ambush because we were in a cease fire, or putting a weapon to a kid's head, or burning down a village that had been hostile, or killing a wounded soldier who had a weapon in his hand, or inadvertently killing women and children that had been caught up in a combat situation? There was no moral dilemma here for most of us.

In non-combat situations it was a little different. The torturing of a prisoner to death did not sit well but after it happened there was no great moral outcry. We just knew it should not have happened. The girls coming through the fence were not killed, we stopped it but if they were killed I am sure no one would have testified at his court martial if they even had one. He was one of us.

The four kids that were killed, I am sure we all felt sorry for them and their mothers, but I am equally sure that everyone was glad nothing happened to the guy that did it.

As for the ecstasy that is felt when killing the enemy I am glad it was a one time thing for me. Not something that continued to grow but I am not sure that was the case with everyone. Taking the life of another human being affected everyone in one way or another.

In Vietnam your moral values changed. No combat soldier left Vietnam with the same moral values they brought with them. This became one of the big problems veterans had in adjusting to civilian life. Once again there had to be a transformation in their moral values, so that they could comply with values of our so-called normal society. While trying to come to terms with this transformation is where I feel a lot of veterans got lost.

You went from, "thou shalt not kill" to "thou shalt kill" and when returning to the states we were supposed to automatically go back to our original moral concepts. It just cannot work that way. The moral values that were instilled in us from our youth to one degree or another had changed. To be asked to blindly accept them again was naive; there were questions, many questions. Most of us had to reevaluate our beliefs. This took some time. We had to form a new set of moral beliefs. While the new set of moral beliefs may or may not have differed that much from the original it was getting there that presented problems. To accept the concepts of religion, authority, war, life, death, drugs, sex, relationships, work ethics, race, life style, and conformity could not be done by accepting someone else's beliefs on these matters. We had to form our own understanding.

Unfortunately in doing so many veterans formed conclusions that led them in the wrong direction. It is much easier to believe in something that appears to be morally right because you were taught it was that way than to question the fundamental integrity of something and form your own beliefs. We are all human. We are all capable of making errors in judgment.

Attitude

The attitude that you have, that is the way you feel toward something, can be influenced by many variables.

There was one basic attitude that I brought with me when I was drafted into the army. I was never a gung-ho, rah-rah, let's go army type of person. I was drafted, planned to do my two years honorably but as inconspicuously as possible.

One day towards the end of my A.I.T. (advanced infantry training), I was called into the captain's office. "Sit down soldier. You have been selected as the leading candidate for trooper of the cycle. Do you know what that means?"

"No sir."

"Every class we select one soldier whose performance, character and attitude best exemplifies the standards of an American soldier. Do you think you qualify for this honor?"

"Thank you very much for considering me. I am sure this is a great honor but I don't want to be trooper of the cycle."

He looked at me with astonishment. "That's all soldier, return to your duty."

The next afternoon I was again called into the captain's office. This time there was the captain, my lieutenant, my drill sergeant and the chaplain. I was hit with a barrage of questions. "We understand that you do not want to be trooper of the cycle. Do you know what an honor it is to be selected?"

"Don't you think your parents would be proud of you?"

"Why would you turn this down?"

"You'll be promoted to an E4."

"Your ratings are the highest of anyone in camp."

"You maxed most of the tests."

"Your physical education scores are in the top ten percent."

"You have no behavioral or attitude problems."

"Could you tell us why you feel this way?"

Their attitudes ranged from bewildered to annoyed.

"I mean no disrespect here. I am sure that my parents would be proud of this accomplishment. I am not a career soldier. I did not volunteer to be in the army, I just want to serve my time and get out. I do not enjoy being here. The training at times is degrading and almost intolerable. I do not want your awards."

I stayed very calm. It felt good to get that off of my chest but I was not sure of the consequences. The sergeant started yelling. The lieutenant was indignant, the chaplain was not sure what to do, and the captain did not say a word. I just kept wondering if I should have just kept my mouth shut. I did not say another word. The sergeant yelled, "You want degrading, I'll show you degrading."

The captain looked at me, "You are dismissed soldier."

They continued to talk as I left the room. I knew that I had just made a mistake. After nearly sixteen weeks in the army, I knew better than to open my mouth but much to my surprise nothing happened. I even got a pass that weekend. I think I gained the respect of the captain but I really was not sure. I kept my mouth shut through the remaining time there, then it was home on leave and off to Vietnam.

I guess my father's departing words, "Be a good soldier, but don't be a hero" were basically reflective of my attitude towards the army.

Besides personal attitudes, army units themselves had their own attitude. The 82nd Airborne was a proud unit that engulfed the persona of being tough. Most units in Vietnam wore combat neutral colors to designate their unit on their uniforms, not the 82nd Airborne. We wore the bright red, white and blue insignia of our unit on our uniforms. The feeling was that they wanted the enemy to know with whom they were dealing. This is the

82nd Airborne, you mess with us, you'll have hell to pay for it. This attitude was especially pronounced during the time we spent up north in I core. Soldiers would have ripped the patches off their uniforms and placed them on the dead Vietnamese soldiers, sort of like saying, "Yeah, we killed them, now what are you going to do about it?" At first I wondered if this was the best strategy but you accepted it. You became part of the unit.

The airborne soldiers especially the officers were very gung-ho. The first captain that I had was an airborne ranger. He wanted to be in the war. Our lieutenant who came a couple of weeks after I had been in country, was a West Point graduate, airborne ranger. He was a good man but gung-ho as hell. Between them they volunteered us for every mission they could get their hands on. It was usually alpha company first because of the captain and first platoon on point because of the lieutenant. It bothered you a little that we always seemed to be first but you accepted it, there was not much else that you could do about it, so you became part of it.

There used to be a saying that we had, which a lot of soldiers believed to be true, "Yea though I walk through the valley of the shadow of death, I fear no evil, for I am the evilest mother-fucker in the valley."

This was the image that the 82nd wanted and for the most part is what it got. I always knew that I was tough although I never wanted to be labeled as a tough guy but to be part of a unit that projected itself as being tough was good. It gave you confidence.

There was a general that periodically flew out to the field. It might sound hard to believe but he used to give us pep talks like a football coach at half time. "You guys are doing a good job, we are all proud of you. This is the best unit in all of Vietnam!"

He usually came out after we had been involved with some kind of contact with the enemy. "I want to let you know that I am no armchair general. Your grunts are the backbone of this army, I am with you all the way."

As silly as this may sound you felt good when he came out to the field, at least most of the time.

One day after we were involved in some light contact, the general flew out to give Charlie company his spiel. He was on his way to us next, but there was nowhere for his helicopter to land. My squad was sent to Charlie company to escort the general back to our position.

The only quick access between us was through a riverbed. It was really more like a small stream running through the mountains. I was walking slack (second man). There were only eight or nine of us. I looked around at the terrain, what a perfect spot for an ambush. There were small cliffs on both sides of the stream. We knew Charlie (Vietnamese soldiers) was in the area. Here we were only squad size, walking the most important officer in the 82nd through the bush. We got there without incident. He gave us his pep talk, we had to escort him back.

We knew that the Vietnamese sources of intelligence were good. What could be better than killing a general? I was thinking that this was crazy. Why was this man putting himself in such a position? If he was worried you sure could not tell it. We reached Charlie company. He thanked us. He said that he had never seen a squad move with such precision and such professionalism. On the way back, I was thinking that it felt good to be patted on the back but I wished to hell he would stay in the rear rather than to go through this again.

Although it wasn't my choice, being with a unit that conducted itself in this type of military manner was reassuring and eventually, as long as I had to be there anyway, I was glad that I was assigned to the 82nd Airborne.

Sometimes, however, the gung-ho-ness would border on the ridiculous. One night we were set up in a company sized N.D.P. on a hill, about three mountain peaks down from our position we were watching mortar fire from Charlie being directed at another unit. The captain got on the radio, "We spotted mortar fire at this location, I am going to take my men and pursue the enemy."

He must have received a negative answer from the other end. He started yelling, "I want them, they're mine." After carrying on almost like a little kid, it became apparent that someone on the line had a little sense and was not letting him go. He was pissed.

The rest of us were happy. To move at night was no easy task but to go that distance into a hostile area, at night, bordered on suicidal.

The airborne units were not the only gung-ho units there. The Marines were also in the area. We worked only one joint operation with Marines. We were to act as a blocking force as the Marines swept towards our direction. It was a Marine operation. A cadre of Marines were assigned to our unit. On the way we encountered sniper fire. It was too great of a distance for our weapons to be effective. Our captain was about to call for air support. The Marine officers protested. I was about twenty yards away. "You cannot call in the Airforce for one lousy sniper, we have a mission to accomplish. Our guys will get him."

The captain never made the call. As far as I was concerned I would call in the whole damned Airforce for one lousy sniper.

Now I do not know if the Marine officers thought that by calling in air support they would jeopardize the mission or that they had such an attitude that they were averse to calling the Airforce unless they were desperately needed. I had the feeling that it was the latter. I have a high respect for the Marine Corps but if their attitude was that they were Marines and they could handle the situation, you only call for air support when it is absolutely, last resort, necessity. I was glad to be with the 82nd Airborne.

The northern section of South Vietnam by its very nature helped foster some of the attitudes. You had very little contact with the people. The enemy you faced was regular army soldiers. You became a little callous. You did not have day to day contact with civilization. You spent most of the time in the field. There were times when you did not even know what day it was. I do not mean the date. You did not know if it was Monday, Tuesday or Friday. Your main concentration was fighting the war, seeking out and destroying the enemy, there were little social amenities.

All this changed when we went down south. It was almost like being in two different wars.

One of the first days out in the field after being located west of Saigon can help illustrate this point. We were on patrol and had stopped to take a break. Two Vietnamese girls came up to us with satchels containing cold beer and soda. They were trying to sell it to us for fifty cents a piece.

"Who are these girls? What do they have? Check them out. Make sure they are not armed."

"Sarge, they have cold beer and soda, they want to sell it to us."

We confiscated it. One of the girls protested loudly. She went after the guy with the satchels. He smacked her, knocking her to the ground. He walked away. She got up and started going after him. The next thing you heard was bullets entering the chambers, everyone was locking and loading their sixteens.

"Get out of here before we kill you."

The rifles were pointed at the girls. They got scared and ran away.

"Could you imagine that, these girls are trying to sell us our own beer and soda for fifty cents a piece? They're lucky we did not shoot them for highway robbery. Hey Joe, I think she liked you. Did you see the way she went after him?"

"I might give her fifty cents for her body but for beer or soda? Anybody thirsty?"

A couple of days later you would have thought that we committed the crime of the century. The girls must have gotten to some high ups. They in turn came out to our area to yell at us.

"Where do you guys think you are? What are you animals? This is not up north. You have to treat these people with respect, it is their country and we are invited guests. Anymore incidents like the other day and you will be court-martialed. Any question?"

We could hardly believe what we were hearing. We knew that we were in for a different type of war.

My attitude also started to change but not for the better. During the transition from north to south there was about a three-week period where they had nothing for us to do. They had us set up in a rear area base camp. An extremely secure area. We did not even have weapons. Outside of the perimeter of the camp, about one hundred yards, was a house of ill repute. It was off limits to all members of the 82nd. Could you imagine, I had been in country for over four months, many a lot longer, we had hardly even seen a woman, no less been with one. They let a whore house exist directly across from the compound then tell us we couldn't go there. Naturally we did not comply with these rules. As luck might have it the first time I went there they were raided by M.P.'s. They put us all in jail then turned us over to our unit. They gave us all article 15's, busted us in rank, and gave us some menial bullshit task to perform. I was busted from a PFC, E3, to a private E2. I was pissed. I really did not care about rank but after what we had been through up north it was insulting and I let them know how I felt.

The first day back out in the field they gave me the RTO's extra battery to carry as some type of menial punishment. At first I refused to carry it. I told them it was crazy. What happens if we become separated because of a fire fight and the RTO's battery goes dead? We'll lose communication and if you think I am going to run across a battlefield to give him his battery, think again. The lieutenant started giving me all sorts of bull. I told him that he was wrong, as an E2 I was not even supposed to be out in the field. I took the battery.

That day was a hot sunny day. After three weeks of lounging in the rear, the sun was starting to get to me. The whole day was getting to me. The lieutenant had us walking through rice paddies rather than on the dike surrounding them. We spent hours doing this.

"Lieutenant, why don't we walk on the dikes?"

"No, they might be booby trapped."

"Lieutenant, the Vietnamese are walking on them, they are not booby trapped," but he was stubborn.

The heat was starting to get to me. I was getting dizzy. I went to the medic and told him I was sunstroke that I wanted to leave the field. The medic told the lieutenant. The lieutenant wouldn't call for a chopper. The medic had the authority but wouldn't buck the lieutenant. We went on for about a half an hour. The medic helped me with some equipment. They finally called for a medivac. It was the first and only time that I was ever medivaced from the field.

Being an E2 started bothering me. It's not that there was that much difference between an E2 and an E3, and I was never looking for a rank, it's just that it was degrading. I was a good soldier and by now a seasoned combat veteran. There were cherries that out ranked me. I did not like the way I was being treated. About a week later we were setting up a company sized N.D.P., our squad was set overlooking a small river. We had a new captain. My partner was on guard, the captain was coming around to check the positions. I was about to go to sleep. The captain asked my partner, "Where are your claymores?"

He did not know what to say, he shook me, "Hey Danny, where are our claymores?"

I was going to say that we usually did not negotiate a river to set claymores on the other side but instead I looked the captain right in the eye and said "I am only an E2. Why are you asking me?" The captain was speechless. He made the squard leader cross the river and set up claymores. I went back to sleep.

We went back to the fire base about three days later. Orders were waiting for me, reinstating me as a P.F.C. I felt like I had won a battle. My attitude returned to normal.

The next two to three months were peaceful. With the exception of being fired at by a machine gun one night, you would not have known you were in a war. Up north was different. Even when you were not involved you knew there was a war taking place. You would hear the B52's dropping bombs at night. You would watch the airforce drop napalm. Sometimes you could sit back in the mountains and watch a battle take place two or three clicks away. You would watch the gun ships lighting up the area.

For the first couple of months down south we did nothing. We went on patrols and set ambushes but there was no enemy. We were not complaining, it was just very different. Your attitude also became different, we started to become complacent. For myself even more so, I was in country five or six months at the time. This was a period where a lot of soldiers slacked off. Even in bad areas. I am not really sure why. It had something to do with adjusting to your surroundings. You were no longer a scared kid you were the first couple of months but you weren't a short timer either.

You were past the beginning, you couldn't see the end, you were just there. This time came for me at a time when for all practical purposes we were not involved in a combat situation. I really began to slack off. I was probably lucky to be in such a peaceful area, but as they say, all good things must come to pass.

We moved from there down to the Macong Delta region. The war was real again and the attitudes changed. Even though by now most of the regular airborne personnel had gone home. We became the 82nd Airborne again.

We were taking over a base camp, I believe from the ninth infantry, when our lieutenant made us double time in formation through the area. The people in the 'ninth' looked at us like we had two heads but you could feel a spirit building. We were once again a force to be reckoned with and unfortunately combat again was no stranger.

One day our lieutenant, a new man to the field, was wounded. He had a small piece of shrapnel in his leg, I really do not recall the circumstances but we probably had been mortared. We also had a new captain, a gung-ho southerner. It was his second tour in nam. The Lieutenant wanted to be medivaced from the field. The captain looked at the wound and said, "That's nothing, you can make it with us to the N.D.P. I thought the airborne was supposed to be tough."

The medic said nothing. The lieutenant walked with us to the N.D.P.

A few days later when we got back to the fire base, I layed into the medic.

"What's wrong with you? Are you afraid of the captain? Why didn't you medivac the lieutenant out of there?"

"Well the captain did not authorize it."

"Don't give me that shit, you're supposed to look out for us. If we can't count on you, who the hell can we count on? You did the same thing to me a couple of months back. You wouldn't medivac me out of the field for sun stroke. You have the authority."

"Well I helped you with your gear, didn't I, and eventually got you out of the field."

"I am glad you carried my gear, I wasn't even sunstroke that day, you have no balls, fuck you!" Then I walked away.

It is not a smart thing for an infantry soldier to get on the wrong side of a medic but I was pissed. Doc, if you ever happen to read this, I really was sunstroke. When I got back to the rear my muscles cramped up the size of cantaloupes. As a medic in combat situations you were great.

You started to develop an attitude that you did not care. If there was something you did not like you weren't going to put up with it. You developed an attitude of, "What are they going to do to me, send me to Vietnam? I'm already here. Send me to the field? Likewise. There is nothing worse that you can do to me than what I am experiencing now, nothing." It gave you a sense of independence. Nobody was going to mess with you and for the most part they didn't. Even the officers realized. What could they do? Threaten you with a court martial? Send you to LBJ? (Longbien Jail). It was better than being out in the field. I don't mean that there was a break down in discipline because there wasn't. Everyone realized what they had to do when they were in the field, but do not mess with me, you really do not have the upper hand. If we hit contact we will be in the same fire fight together, bullets are flying everywhere, who knows where one might go?

I never saw one American Soldier shoot another out of malice but the possibility existed.

We were now seasoned veterans, nobody had to tell us what to do, we knew. We knew more than the rookie officers and N.C.O.'s that they started sending to the field. We started to get short. Our survival depended upon the unit acting as professionals. If there were any problems we would deal with them ourselves.

Being out in the field was a miserable existence. You were either hot or wet or tired. You had to deal with fear, death, the enemy, the elements, just so many different things, it's a wonder that we maintained one composure.

It is hard to understand the miserable existence that you experienced as a combat infantry soldier but let me give you a small comparison. I was watching television the other night, it was about rabid raccoons making their way up north. People were frantic, they were holding town meetings, they were all afraid that if they were attacked that they would have to get rabies shots. The fear of getting a needle in the stomach for a few days at a time was a prime concern, almost devastating to some.

One day we were out in the field when we stopped to set up an N.D.P. Somehow one of the soldiers was scratched by a rat. He went to the medic. The next day he was medivaced to the rear. About a month later he came back to the field. Everyone was glad to see him.

"I'll bet it hurt getting a needle everyday."

"Are you kidding? There was a little pain once a day, but then I got to live like a normal person. Hot meals, showers, liquor, women. I had to report to the hospital every morning then I spent the rest of the day in Saigon. I hope the rat comes back and scratches me again tonight."

Within a week there were twenty or so soldiers who mysteriously came down with rat scratches out of our company alone. We started with less than one hundred men, now we were down to about seventy. I considered it but it just was not my way of doing things.

The 82nd Airborne came up with a solution. They brought all the men back out to the field and told them they were going to fly the vaccine out every day. They would get their rabies shot in the field, by the next day the problem was over. No one went for their shots. Nothing was ever said.

Most people would do anything to get out of the field. We all hoped to get a million dollar wound just bad enough to take us out of the field but no permanent damage done. There were even people with more serious wounds that were happy with them rather than be out in the field.

With the exception of the rat scratches and one guy who blew his own head off, I never saw a self-inflicted wound but I am sure they happened. The day that we dug foxholes and were being mortared I was told that one guy stuck his leg up the whole time hoping to get wounded. He was not lucky enough.

There was one fiasco that really affected my attitude. I was in country seven or eight months at the time. They came down with an order that stated, anyone who is scheduled to deros (leave country) in June either had to extend their tour to the following month or they would be reassigned back up north with 101st Airborne. The reasoning was that there were too many of us leaving in June and they did not want to have a unit comprised mostly of cherries.

My first reaction was that there was no way that I would extend my tour even one hour but there was a lot to consider. Going back up north was not an ideal situation. We did nothing there but hump up and down mountains all day. You were constantly exhausted. There were some days that you reached the mountain peak, you swore that if you were attacked that you would not have the energy to fight back. I am sure that the adrenaline would start pumping but it was a miserable existence. You lived better down south. There were hot meals, cold beer, women, Saigon when you got the chance, just a different life style. You were also tired down south. When you were out in the field you did not sleep more than two or if you were lucky three hours at a time. You humped the bush all day long but it was not up and down mountains. You were only in the field four to seven days at a time before you came back to a fire base. As far as safety was concerned it was about even. Up north you faced the N.V.A. but down south there were booby traps and the VC who could harass the hell out of you.

The most compelling argument was, what happens if during the extended time you get killed or maimed, had your legs blown off or became a vegetable for the rest of your life. On the other hand most of the guys you were with you had been with for a long time. You knew each other. You knew you were with a good outfit. If you did go up north, what happened if you were killed or maimed, had your legs blown off or became a vegetable? If you survived you would be second-guessing yourself for the rest of your life.

You knew what you had, you did not know where you were going. It was the toughest decision I ever made in my life. I extended ten days.

Most of the guys extended, some did not. Some extended into August and September so they would get out of the service when their tour was over. I would have had to extend till August 23rd. It was not even a consideration.

One month went by, nearly two months went by and nobody was being transferred up north. I began to inquire. I went from the captain to as high up as I could go, nobody said anything. Finally one day in the rear I got a hold of a clerk. "You did not get this from me but because of all the extensions there was no need to send anyone up north."

I was fuming. I tried to get my extension revoked. No way. I wrote home. It was suggested that I write to Congressman Murphy, I guess because there was an Irish connection. Not only did he not investigate the matter he wrote a letter to my captain suggesting that he had a trouble maker under his command and that he should deal with me in the proper manner. The first sergeant and the captain started to break my chops but to no avail they could not shut me up. They threatened me with a court martial. I dared them. I told them I wanted this out in the open. They told me that if I did not keep quiet they would not give me my army accommodation medal or my Bronze Star. I told them what they could do with them, I just wanted my extension revoked. I got nowhere fast. I wrote to everyone from the President on down. I even stopped some big wig general, I think it was Abrams, who had come to look at some prisoners we had taken back to a fire base. He would take the matter under consideration. The only person who responded in a favorable manor was Congressman Emanuel Cellers. By the time he got to investigate what was going on, it was too late. My tour of duty was almost over but I appreciated his effort. I was not the only one affected by this but I yelled the loudest. The rest let me carry the ball for whatever good it did.

The joke became what can you do, send me to Vietnam? Yeah, and extend my tour. You might think something like this would affect you in the field, it didn't. You learned to separate the bullshit from your basic goal of survival. Especially then because I was a short timer.

Years later, when Congressman Murphy was indicted and send to jail, I went out, got drunk, and celebrated.

Whatever the circumstances were, being in Vietnam created a distinct attitude. That's why when most veterans returned to the world they were accused of having attitude problems. I am going to deal with this in another chapter.

My overall attitude of being a good soldier, but not being a hero, never really changed but my perception of what it was to be a good soldier or a hero changed immensely from the time I landed in country until the time I left.

There were a lot of factors that contributed to your attitude but the most compelling was death. Death affected you on many levels and in many different ways. The fear of death was most intense during your first couple of months. After that it was not that you were not afraid of dying but you learned to live with the possibility. You faced death, it was still a fear, but it lessened in magnitude. Even when you became short the level of fear that was in you rose, but your attitude towards death was different, it was not based on a fear of death. Not that you necessarily got callous towards death, it was something that existed. It was there, it happens. You did everything that you could to survive but you accepted the reality of death. Death still affected you but the fear of dying became a different reality, you learned to face death.

Death itself was very personal. It affected people in different ways. Some people would laugh about it, some would become ghoulish about it, some seemed indifferent, everyone had to deal with it in his own way. The immediate death of a fellow soldier, was almost universally dealt with in the same manner. You wanted to kill the son of a bitch who did it. You wanted to kill anyone who was associated with them and you really did not care who got in the way. You wanted revenge and you wanted it now.

That's why fighting in a war that you could not always distinguish between the civilians and the enemy I am surprised that there were not a lot more civilians killed.

They say that death is the ultimate reality but being involved with death did not really help you in understanding it. It only made the act of dying and the fact that at anytime you may be dead an immediate reality, although for the most part you really did not dwell on it. Death was still the same reality but your fear of death had changed.

The fear of death became similar to the act described in an earlier chapter about crossing the bridge. The first time I crossed the bridge the fear was almost intolerable. The next time crossing, although the fear was still there, it had transcended into a different reality. I already faced this fear and facing it again would never be as intense as the initial crossing. The fear would probably always be there but it mitigated in intensity. Facing death was similar, however I am not sure what the cumulative effect of facing death day after day had on the human psyche. I am sure that there is a quotient of death that any human being can tolerate but what that quotient is probably is unique to each individual. If you surpass that individual quotient there are many psychological and emotional factors that can evolve. Even if you do not fill that individual quotient where death becomes intolerable, the experience of facing death and the cumulative effect of facing death upon death upon death for better or worse will change you forever.

Facing death affects your attitude in many ways but it was not always the most dominant factor. One day there was a company sized combat assault, I was in country about ten months at the time and we were working the Delta region. We boarded the choppers just before dawn. Our platoon was in the lead. As they set down, hovering a few feet off the ground, we jumped off the choppers into a rice paddy. Normally a rice paddy has one to two feet of water in them but when we disembarked we landed in water that was up to our shoulders. It was a hot L.Z., we were taking fire. There was not much we could do. We took cover by the dike, still immersed in the water, and returned fire but we could not see the enemy. The choppers took off and then second set advanced with the soldiers disembarking into an adjacent rice paddy. Same scenario. They were immersed in water and taking fire. It was determined that the L.Z. was too hot for any other choppers to advance.

There we were immersed in water and immobile with sporadic fire coming in our direction. Helicopter gun ships were called in. They lit up the area in front of us firing machine guns, rockets, and whatever else was in their arsenal, the enemy firing stopped. The gun ship left. We were in a strange position. To the north was a river, beyond that river was where the firing came from. In every other direction were similar rice paddies to the one we were in. As we started to move more enemy fire rained down on us. We called for gun ships. They lit up the area, the enemy stopped firing. We tried to move and they started firing, we called in gun ships, this went on all day.

Charlie, wherever he was, must have been dug in so when the gun ships arrived his position was secure, rendering the gun ships ineffective. He was also far enough away from us that their firing was ineffective. No one was hit. You either heard bullets going over your head or saw them fall short in the water in front of you. The closest I saw were a couple that had hit a dike a few feet away from me.

The officers were on the horn all day trying to figure out what to do. Hours went by. It was noon it became late afternoon. We did not move all day. There we stayed immersed in water, sun beating down and no one seemed to be doing anything.

Our lieutenant, who was in country only a couple of months, seemed to be the one in command. By now it was maybe two hours before dusk. They seemed to be formulating a decision that we were going to spend the night there and that there would be some kind of combat assault the next morning that would sweep towards the area. Why there was no immediate decision on what to do or how to do it I never really understood.

I told the lieutenant that we could not stay there all night. They knew our position and if they had mortars or rockets they would annihilate us. We had to move. We began to argue. We were both tired, wet, uncomfortable and frustrated. I told him that he was an asshole and that he was going to get us all killed.

"Whose stupid fucking idea was it to land here in the first place? You had all day to figure something out. What the fuck are you doing?"

He was pissed. "If you got any better ideas, you get us out of here."

"All right I will."

I looked over the area that we had been looking at all day. About three hundred and fifty to four hundred yards to the southeast looked to be high ground. I took a cherry as my slack man and started to get the hell out of there. I got about ten yards when I got up on top of a dike. Bullets whistled by my head, I dove down onto the dike. I looked at my arm and it was black, covered with ants. I submerged myself into the water and brushed them off. A fairly new sergeant to the field yelled for me to stay down. "You are going to get yourself killed."

I thought about it for a minute. There should have been a fear in me and there was but at that point I was more tired and frustrated than scared. Besides, I felt if I did not get us out of there we were not going to get out of there. I knew what the sergeant was saying was right but at that point I knew I was going to go on. It's not that I was callous towards death. I did not want to die but what were the options. If we stayed there our chances of dying were good. Besides, somehow I knew I was not going to die in Vietnam, or was that just wishful thinking? There was some more sporadic gunfire but it really did not come close to hitting us.

I turned to my slack man and asked if he was ready to go on. He looked at me and said, "I am with you." The two of us proceeded. No one else. We stayed in the water, working our way east then south along an adjacent dike. I came upon a small break in the dike and went over to the next rice paddy. Now the water was over our heads. We clung upon the dike working our way south. I turned to my slack man and asked if he was all right. He had only been in the field a couple of weeks. He just kept saying, "I'm with you."

We kept working our way south when I hit a dike running east that was submerged about four feet. We followed the dike toward the high ground. While walking along this dike through the water, all of a sudden there was a break in the dike. I felt it but it was too late. I was under water. The weight of my ruck sack was holding me down. I managed to find the dike and get myself up. I instinctively turned to my slack man and asked if he was all right. He shook his head there was a smile on his face, sort of a sign of relief. "Am I all right, still shaking his head, I'm with you." I helped him negotiate the break in the dike, then paused for a minute. Barring any further breaks I saw a way to the high ground. I turned to the rest of the platoon or two platoons, however many had landed and signaled for them to proceed and at the same time, showing them by pointing downward that there was a break in the dike. They were a couple of hundred yards away so I was hoping that they understood. We had no radio with us.

We started to proceed and a fear started to come over me. Maybe the dunk in the water brought me back to my senses. There were no bullets flying but the fact that I had almost drowned, the two of us standing in the middle of nowhere in essence by ourselves, we were going towards high ground which was ripe for an enemy ambush, all started running through my mind. My adrenaline started pumping.

We reached the high ground. The two of us checked out the area. It was clean. We moved to the best vantage point, released our ruck sacks and sat down. I lit up a cigarette. It amazed me that they were dry. I kept them sealed in an empty grenade canister.

About an hour later my lieutenant reached our position, he looked at me. I really do not know what I was expecting him to say, but what came out of his mouth shocked me. There was no thank you, no good job, no pat on our back for saving our ass. Instead he said, "You look well rested, go help the other guys." I looked at him and said, "Fuck you!" He did not say a word. I got up and went down toward the rice paddy, no one really needed my help. With the exception of the guys in my squad nobody even thanked me. Not one officer, not one sergeant. If it had been anyone else they would have given them the silver star. I have seen people get it for a lot less. By this point in time my attitude was wrong for the army's way of thinking. I was too independent. I still took orders but if something bothered me, I let them know it. After all, this was my life, I was a short timer. Less than two months to go and you already fucked me for ten days. From that day on my attitude was simple. I wanted to stay alive and I wanted out of the field. I told them that I would no longer walk point or flank with an M79. I wanted an M16. The M79 only shot one bullet at a time. I wanted more protection. They ordered me to walk flank one day and I gave them a hard time. Initially I refused unless they gave me a 16. They threatened disciplinary action and court-martials and whatever the hell else. Whatever you are going to do to me is going to get me out of the field. I had enough. I walked flank with the 79 because deep down I did not want the disgrace of what this type of court-martial would bring. The next cherry that came out to the field got my 79 and I got a 16.

My attitude towards the army was now almost one of contempt. I was a good soldier in the field but that was not enough. They were playing games and they realized that it was with my life and the lives of everyone over there.

The next time we were back at a fire base I smoked a bowl and thought just what the hell was going on. Why wasn't this war over? I had never been in a battle that we lost. When we were up north we chased the N.V.A. through the Ashue Valley and seemingly completely out of I Corp through the D.M.Z. and then stopped. We chased them to the Cambodia border and some of the element of the 82nd even went into Cambodia and then stopped. It seemed that we would pursue the enemy and win the battles but only go so far. Was it all just a game? Now the only thing I wanted was out of the field, and eventually with the help of the lieutenant I did just that.

My attitude towards the army, the war, and life in general had evolved to a point that was completely different from that which I had when I had entered the country. In spite of how all this might sound, I was not a hard case or a complainer or even someone who walked around with a negative attitude. I had always been outspoken but I respected and even was submissive to authority. The respect and the submissiveness had changed to the point where I could no longer have blind respect for authority and being submissive was no longer part of my nature but more than that had changed.

One day we were back at a base camp. This was one of the few times that they put us in an area that had tents and cots and a mess tent. It was like living in luxury. It was near the end of my tour. I was sitting on a cot cleaning my weapon, an M16, when I heard an argument coming from the next tent. I looked to see what was going on. All the tents had the sides rolled up and were encased by a three to four foot wall of sandbags. There was a cherry from the second platoon yelling at one of the regulars. All of a sudden there was gunfire. The cherry shot a burst of rounds into the sandbags. Everyone scattered. My adrenaline started pumping. I calmly went to the end of the tent, positioned myself behind the sandbags, locked and loaded my 16, and took dead aim at the cherry. There was not much of a thought process involved. If he made another move to use his weapon in a manner that could even remotely hurt someone I was going to blow him away. He had a scared look on his face, very unstable, I continued to have him in my sights. A few people came into the tent and started yelling at him. Finally someone took the weapon away. I lowered my 16 and went back to my cot. I do not think anyone saw what I was doing.

I thought about the situation for a while. The people who disarmed the cherry handled it in the proper manner. Out of the options available to me I chose the one that would have ended his life. Why? I was not abnormally scared, I was not some psycho who was looking to kill, I personally was in no immediate danger, I guess I was looking to protect my fellow soldier but this man was also a fellow soldier. Had my attitude come to a point where under certain circumstances the taking of a man's life was no big deal? As I knelt behind the sandbags with this man in my sights there was no doubt about what I would have done, not even a second thought. I know that if he had shot someone or even attempted to shoot someone that the taking of his life would have been justified but why was this the option I chose? How much had I changed? The realization of what had happened was scary. What has this war done to me?

Military Intelligence: A Contradiction In Terms?

When we were in basic training the sergeants used to have a saying, there are three ways to do something. The right way, the wrong way, and the army way and you are in the army.

I guess it meant that it did not matter whether the army way was right or wrong. It was the way things were going to be done.

One day when we were out in the field, I was in country about two months at the time, we were working in the I Corp area near the Ashue valley. They had gathered us around for an intelligence briefing. The night before camp eagle, our base area, was attacked by sappers. Sappers were sort of semi-suicidal squads that would infiltrate an area, set off satchel charges, grenades, open fire, and in the chaos try to retreat from the area. In this instance there were several prisoners taken. They had revealed an area where the North Vietnamese army had their base camp.

We were sent on a search and destroy mission, we were working in a battalion sized operation, roughly five companies. The military must have looked upon this information as highly reliable. They moved us in an extremely swift manner. By the next morning they had landed us in a clearing with three mountain peaks surrounding us. Our company advanced toward the top of one of the mountain peaks. Advancing up the side of a mountain can be a very difficult and dangerous endeavor. There is rarely a direct path to the top. You move in single file toward your objective. If the enemy has secured the area they have a distinct advantage. They have the best vantage point. If you hit contact you are basically only fighting them with a few soldiers at a time, making it impossible to gain superiority in fire power. You must gain superiority in fire power in order to win a battle. The casualties that you can incur could be astronomical, thus the expression, fighting an uphill battle.

We reached the peak without contact. There were eight to ten huts on this peak. We searched the huts. There was food on the mats and in some huts the food was still cooking, everything was still hot. We had surprised the enemy and they left in a hurry. They did not even take time out to booby trap anything. We searched the huts looking for contraband, they were clean.

We were standing around the camp, ready to move out, when one of the guys stepped into something. The ground appeared to break under his foot. As he pulled his foot out you could see something under the ground, it was a case of rifles. They removed the case but there was another then another. We had stumbled upon what was at the time, and maybe still, the largest cache of armament ever found in Vietnam. There were hundred upon hundreds of cases of rifles. There were cases of machine guns, grenades, rockets, RPG's, anti-tank weapons, mines, anti-personnel mines, ammunition and uniforms. The amount of armament buried in the ground was staggering, it took us days to get it all out.

It was amazing to see this. All brand new Chinese made weapons still in the cases in which they were manufactured. All the rifles were taken back to the rear. We each got one to take home. The rest of the munitions were piled in an area about half the size of a football field and about as high up as we could stack them.

How the Vietnamese got these weapons here is hard to figure. We were on a mountaintop in the middle of a mountain range away from everything. The ground on top of the cache looked undisturbed. They were ingenious people.

We uncovered weapons I had never seen or even heard of before. There was something that one of the sergeants called a bouncing Betty mine. He explained the effect like this, picture having a case of grenades, some with five second fuses, some ten second, some twenty second, and rolling them down the mountain. Could you imagine what that would do to any troops on the mountain?

You began to think. What if the Vietnamese had decided to stay and fight? What if they had spotted us landing and set up an ambush? We all would have been history.

How could the military have run such an operation? They were fairly certain of the intelligence that they had received from the prisoners, yet, there were no artillery strikes, no Air Force bombardment, and no B52 strikes. They sent the ground troops in first to fight what would have been an uphill battle against a highly armed North Vietnamese army. We could have been annihilated, then they would have bombarded with artillery and sent in the airforce.

Was there any planning or coordination going on? Was there an overall strategy for these types of situations or was each fending for itself?

Before we left the area the engineers had decided that the amount of munitions that were stored was too large for them to blow up. They had called for air strikes to hit munitions but first we had to leave the area.

We spent the next two weeks humping area looking for the enemy but they were gone. We were returning to our original L.Z. We walked through the same N.V.A. base camp, when lo and behold, there was all the munitions still intact. There was no airforce strike. What were these people in the rear area doing? Was there any coordination or communication? Or were they so busy trying to get one of these rifles so they could take one home as a war trophy, to put on the wall of their den, that they forgot about everything else.

Our captain was on the horn giving them hell, explaining where he would shove these munitions if he got the chance. He realized the danger that they put us in and that nobody really seemed to care. We left the area, never to return, I do not know if those munitions ever were destroyed.

Planning for this operation was feeble. Many lives could have been lost but when it suited their purpose they could come up with some intricate plans.

One day our platoon was flown into a village. Actually it was two villages adjacent to each other. They were rather large consisting of perhaps forty huts a piece.

During the briefing, before the mission, we were told that this was a V.C. stronghold. We spent about a week searching the village and patrolling the area. There was not a V.C. within miles, this was a friendly village. The closest we came to anything was the first night just before dawn. We had set up an ambush just outside the village. There was movement in the village headed our way. We saw that it was an old man, he had something in his hand. We stopped him when he left the village. He was startled. He had a hoe in his hand. We searched him. He had no contraband. He wanted to go out and work in the rice paddies. We tried to explain that he could not go out until after dawn. He spoke no English and we spoke very little Vietnamese. He started yelling and motioning towards the rice paddy. We tried to explain, not until the sun came up. It was almost a comical scene. He did not care that there was a war going on, this is what he did every day of his life and this what he was going to do that day. The sun came up, we let him go.

That night we set up an ambush around the rice paddy just in case, nothing went on. Just before dawn the old man came strolling out of the village and went to work in the paddies. When the sun came up, he saw us, but he did not seem startled. He just waved and went on about his business. The war was not going to affect him.

After about a week they pulled us from the village. There was a big operation going on, battalion sized. The rumors were that we were going into Cambodia. Nobody knew. They moved us at night. Our orders were to surround this village. When we set up, we realized that this was the village that we had just left. The whole thing seemed strange. Why were they having a battalion sized operation, very rare, to cordon this village. There was nothing there, we spread the word.

It just so happened that it was the night of the 1969 Super Bowl, the Jets versus the Colts. The game came on the radio about 2:00 A.M. Four or five of us from New York went to one position to listen to the game. Under most circumstances we would never do this, but we knew there was nothing there. The game ended and we went back to our positions. It was just before dawn.

We finally just got settled when there was gun fire a couple of hundred yards down the perimeter. Word had passed down that it was V.C., we were startled. How could we have messed up like this? Nobody said anything. The word came down that this was a joint operation between the army and the airforce. Apparently there were politicians and generals and big wigs that came to Vietnam to watch an operation.

Our squad was sent on patrol. We walked past where the firing took place and we were shocked. There was no V.C., just this poor old man lying there dead. What a shame. I'm sure the intelligence had a ball telling the big wigs how we stopped the V.C. at the perimeter. I wonder what body count they gave them.

We went on patrol and everyone was a little down. Nobody said anything but I am sure we were all thinking of this poor old man lying there dead. There was no reason for this. What were we doing, putting on a show for some armchair jocks, so some rear area general could get their jollies? All of a sudden out of the middle of nowhere was this snake, and I mean a snake. The biggest thing I ever saw. It must have been fifteen to twenty feet long and over two feet in circumference. We must have startled it. It picked its head up. Someone shot at it. Then everyone started shooting at it. I hit it with a shotgun round. It was being hit by 16's but the snake took off. We dropped our ruck sacks and pursued. We were like a bunch of kids trying to get the snake. It was a welcome relief.

The next thing, there were helicopters and gun ships and fighter planes all around. We realized what had happened. The RTO had left his radio when we dropped our ruck sacks. Unprecedented but it happened. They thought we had hit contact there was no communication. They were set up for an operation. They reacted as if we were in a fire fight. The whole thing was really hysterical. The army did not think so. The sergeant and the RTO were busted. The snake got away.

The whole thing made you wonder about our military intelligence and what their priorities were. You started to think that the men in the field were not really one of their top priorities. It was just a game to them.

All this coordination for an operation that they knew and we knew was a hoax. They wanted to hoodwink some big wigs and impress them by showing them what a well organized operation was all about. Too bad all operations weren't this well coordinated. It would be a pleasure to see all that air power within a minute of firing your weapon at the real enemy.

The rear echelon were not the only ones who made questionable decisions.

Orders had come down for us to take over the area from the ninth or the twenty-fifth infantry, I forget. I was in country seven or eight months and they were located in the Delta region. Our platoon was designated as the advance team. We went to the area about a week before the rest of the battalion, it was a very bad area.

When we arrived we got familiar with the fire base. We started talking to the troops there about the area. They told us that we were better off out in the field. Every night, like clockwork, about twenty minutes after dusk they would be mortared. Night time came around and they had something that they called a mad minute, it was really reconnaissance by fire. They would take positions around the perimeter of the camp and fire their weapons out into the darkness. The reason for this action was to keep the enemy away from the camp at dusk. Dawn and dusk were optimal times for attack because your eyes were adjusting to the differences in light thereby making it harder to see.

About twenty minutes later you were hit by a mortar barrage. The next night the same thing occurred. I started to think, it really did not take a military genius to figure out what was going on. Every night they would light up the perimeter with this mad minute. If you ever saw a flash from a rifle at night you would realize how bright it is. Now picture a whole perimeter of a base camp with these muzzle flashes going off simultaneously. It would be like stringing light bulbs around the perimeter and turning them on. The enemy would be able to get a fix on the position, set their sights and fire their mortars with a fair degree of accuracy. I told the lieutenant what I thought was happening. He agreed but to him I guess it was just an academic discussion.

The next night the same thing but this time there was a direct hit on the bunker. Everyone was either killed or wounded. I did not know them, they were from the other unit. One guy who was killed had just come in off the field because he was going home. I was crazy. I sought out their person in charge. He was a major or a captain or a colonel, I do not recall. I explained to him what was going on. He said something to the effect of who the hell are you to tell me how to run my camp, get out of here. I told him that he was killing his men and that he might be killing me and a few other choice words. He walked away. Later my lieutenant came up to me and said that he had talked to the officer and started spouting things about insubordination or whatever. I told him that I did not want to hear it and to do something about the situation.

The next three or four nights the same thing. You cannot imagine the frustration that I felt. How many lives were lost, how many people became cripples because of this stupid policy. Didn't anyone have any brains? Again, you did not have to be a military genius to see what was happening. Even if you did not see it, once it was articulated to them they must have understood. Why didn't they listen, because I was a private and they were officers? Or you don't change policy once it is set? Where was the military intelligence? The whole thing was ridiculous.

Finally the 82nd took over. There were no more mad minutes and thus there was no more mortaring the whole time that we were there. For the most part the officers in the field with the 82nd were highly trained combat officers that did not needlessly risk the lives of their men. Ideally every military intelligence officer, dealing with combat situations, should have combat infantry experience.

Some nights you would be out in the field on ambush and you would receive a call that 'intelligence reports' that there are five hundred Charlie about one hundred yards from your position. At first we would get geared up and put people on one hundred percent alert. Eventually you tended to ignore such calls but in the back of my mind I was always hoping they were not like the boy who cried wolf.

Then there were some serious miscalculations, like the time they sent the 1/505 of the 82nd into Cambodia. It seems that the Vietnamese were frustrating our men in the rear. They would initiate contact and retreat behind the Cambodian boundary where Americans were not allowed to pursue, not with the army, or even artillery.

Someone cooked up an operation that sent the 1/505 across the boundary. They pursued the N.V.A. and there were heavy casualties. We were on standby. The only thing they forgot , or worse did on purpose, was to coordinate with the airforce and artillery. When the troops called for support there was no one there to help. The airforce would not go into Cambodia and the artillery would not fire over the boundary. They left them there naked.

The operation only lasted a few days and we were not called to go but our casualties were numerous. It was a disgrace. They sent the troops there without protection. I wonder if our rear area geniuses relieved their frustrations. How this type of an operation was allowed to take place was mind boggling. Either they were used as guinea pigs by a central military intelligence command or there was no center of command that coordinated activities. It was hard for me to believe that the right hand did not know what the left hand was doing but that just might have been the case. I will never know.

Then there was friendly fire. All of this cannot be blamed on the military intelligence. Mistakes happen like the artillery round that landed in the N.D.P. while we were up north. It was human error. It seems that you have one setting for an illumination round and another setting for a high explosive round for the same area.

They shot an H.E. round on an illumination setting, thus the mistake.

The time we were watching the Airforce pound away at a mountain and we found out later that the 101st was on the mountain and received over one hundred casualties, whose mistake was that? The pilots? The people in the rear? How concerned were they about us? Was it just a game to them , where if they made a mistake they would try to rectify it on their game board? Their mistakes were our lives. Were their realities of war so far removed that they just saw them on paper, or were they just that inept?

Take body counts, the biggest game of the war. Let's say we hit contact and had two dead and six wounded, we swept the area and only found one dead Charlie. We would report that. However, somewhere up the line the ratio would not gel. The captain would not look good so he would make it six dead. The people in the rear would not like the numbers, so they would make it sixteen dead, by the time it got to the final person, it would be six million dead. An exaggeration of course, but the body counts were highly inflated. You began to realize that their main concern was to look good on paper. The lives of the men in the field were secondary and that might be putting too high of a priority on us.

The people with the best intelligence in Vietnam were the "coke girls." We ran into them basically down south in the area between Saigon and Cambodia. They would come out to the field every day to sell us beer and soda. It seems a couple of the girls were assigned to a platoon like it was their own exclusive territory. These were not whores. They only sold us beer and soda, but no matter where we went, there they were. Sometimes we would go on combat assaults and be twenty or thirty clicks away in the middle of nowhere, the coke girls would show up. How they knew where we were was uncanny. Either their head procurer was sleeping with someone in military intelligence or there were kick backs all the way up so they made sure they knew where we were.

The part that was worse was when they did not show up. It seemed every time they did not show up we were involved in contact. They had great intelligence on both sides.

If we had the intelligence network that the coke girls had many lives would have been saved.

To put all the blame on military intelligence is not right. The whole war was ill conceived. Take something that might sound as trivial as a tour of duty. The normal tour of duty was for one year. I do now know how this came about but it was stupid, just when you got a seasoned veteran you send him home. This affected all areas infantry, artillery, airforce, intelligence etc. Not only were you losing an experienced soldier you would lose sight of your goals. You were no longer there to win a war. You were there to survive a year and go home. Winning a war was not your goal. Survival was your goal.

The politicians at home were in the same boat. They got us involved in a war but their policy was not one of winning a war but that of containment. If we hold them here or there or defeat them here or there they hoped eventually to arrive at a political solution. This was nonsense. You either fight a war to win a war or you should not get involved in combat.

Political military intelligence is perhaps the greatest contradiction in terms.

Race

The time when I was in Vietnam the whole country was going through racial change. When I was in A.I.T. Martin Luther King Jr. was assassinated. There was racial tension throughout the camp.

When I arrived in Vietnam, race was the furthest thing from my mind and basically there was little racial tension in the unit in which I served. That does not mean that race was not a factor nor that racism did not exist. It just did not manifest itself to a point that it caused problems.

The first squad that I was assigned to there were three black men out of ten people in the squad. The most of any squad in the platoon. Over all our company consisted of about 15 % black. This was probably the average representation of most combat units that I encountered in Vietnam.

Race among combat infantry soldiers was rarely a factor. I am not saying that everyone loved each other because prejudice and bigotry existed in many individuals, both black and white, but there was a mutual respect that transcended racial prejudice. We were not black soldiers or white soldiers, just soldiers. We depended on each other to stay alive. When working together in the field race was nonexistent. There were, however, racial factors to the Vietnam experience.

One day we were working up north I was in country about a month or two at the time. We came across this small village that was deserted. We were searching this one hut when we found a box hidden in the floor. We opened the box and there were a lot of very important looking papers. We started to look through them. Most were in Vietnamese. Among the papers were maps and what looked to be military designations. Then we same across some leaflets that were in English. There was a picture of an American black POW. The leaflet was propaganda. Its message went something like this: I am so and so from such a unit. I urge all black Americans to put down their arms. We are fighting a war that is not our war. We are fighting on the side of a racist imperialist nation. The Vietnamese are not our enemy they are our brothers, put down your arms. He signed it.

When I read this I was startled. We gave the papers to the lieutenant but I could not get this out of my mind. How this soldier must have been tortured into saying what he was saying. I felt bad for him. It made me realize that I too could become a prisoner of war. The racial implications of the message did not really hit home, then again I was not black. I saw this as pure propaganda and figured everyone would see it that way.

I never saw or even heard of these type of leaflets being distributed but the possibility existed. Was I being too naive about the racial problems that existed?

One day we were back in a rear area fire base and I started throwing a football around with one of the members of my squad. After a while a few more people came, then some more, before you knew it we were involved in a game of touch tackle. I was playing defensive back and offensive tight end. I liked playing football. I started on my high school team. The game was pretty rough but it felt good to play ball again. We drew a crowd from the rest of the camp who were watching us play. At one point, I intercepted a pass and ran it back for a touchdown. Everyone seemed to be cheering. The game ended and people started coming up to me.

"Give him a beer. Did you see how he out ran all those colored boys? We did not know you were so fast."

I did not realize it but I was the only white player on the field. I guess the whites were proud of me because I played such a good game against the blacks and in a way I was representing them. The attention felt good but seemed strange. I did not realize it but at the time throughout a lot of the country blacks and whites did not play ball together.

Then it was time to eat. I was standing in line at the mess tent when the black mess sergeant came up to me.

"Come here. You do not have to wait in line. Give this man anything he wants. Make sure it is fresh. Seconds, thirds if he wants. Any white boy who plays ball with us and takes the punishment that we were giving out deserves the best."

Now I was also a celebrity with the blacks. I did not realize that they were going after me because I was the only white person on the field. I just thought it was a tough game of football.

For the first time in Vietnam, I realized the polarization between the races but for whatever it was worth I ate good and drank good while at that fire base.

It seems that racism did exist but to what extent it is hard to say. Out in the field it was not a factor but when we got to the rear it became more noticeable.

The most blatant form I ever saw was one day back in the rear a bunch of us, black and white, were hanging out having a few beers and just talking. About fifty yards away, all by himself was a southerner, drunk as a skunk, yelling out racial slurs. Nigger this and nigger that. Who do these niggers think they are? He continued his tirade seemingly forever. Nobody seemed to be paying attention to him. After a while, I felt a little embarrassed. I know that it was bothering me, so I could imagine how the blacks must have felt. Still, nobody said anything. Finally I asked, "Doesn't that bother you?"

"Oh that hillbilly? Don't pay any attention to him, you see he doesn't know any better."

The answer that he doesn't know any better was somewhat bewildering. It seemed a little too cavalier. I though for a while. The blacks seemed to be very magnanimous. Could they be that forgiving or were they afraid to act? I couldn't leave it alone. "He is sitting there calling you niggers and you're telling me he doesn't know any better. If I said that you would be all over me."

"You do not understand. If he came over here and said it to us we would be fighting but he is not confronting us. He is drunk and just saying things that his daddy taught him. You see he really does not know any better."

I left it at that. I was still a little puzzled, but I guess I was from a different culture. There were other cultural differences that became apparent.

One day I was talking to this black man in my squad, we were good friends. He was from California and I was from New York. We were discussing differences in people. He said to me, "don't you notice that I do not particularly hang out with Jones and Leaks? They're black and I am black but they are southern country boys. I am from the city. Even though we are from the same race I do not have a lot in common with them. Now don't get me wrong, if an issue came up that was between blacks and whites I would be with them but that doesn't mean that there are not differences among us. Except for blackness I would probably have more in common with you than I do with them."

The conversation was enlightening, until that point I looked upon most blacks as being from the same ilk. After all, especially in the army, blacks seemed to gravitate toward each other. This was particularly apparent stateside. Any time that there was free time for association the blacks would seem to congregate together, in the mess hall, at movies, during breaks, it always seemed to happen. Now conversely it would appear that the whites also congregated together but it was not the same. Even if a white person did not like blacks there did not seem to be a problem with association. If they happened to be in the same area the whites would hang out with whoever was there. They would not usually look to separate themselves from the blacks. The blacks however, seemed to look to separate themselves from the whites. It was a peculiar thing.

That is probably why I looked at blacks as being as one entity. After this conversation I started to realize the differences among blacks, in religion, class, culture, regional up bringing, and even in ethnicity.

One day we were back at a base camp and there were a bunch of blacks having a discussion. One sergeant from the recon platoon seemed to be in the middle of it. They were talking race among themselves. The sergeant seemed to be putting himself above the rest saying that he was of Jamaican descent, therefore different from the American blacks. The discussion got heated, I was an outside observer. The same guy from my squad laid into the sergeant. He said, "Lookee here, you're a nigger just like I'm a nigger just like we all are niggers. Don't go putting yourself above anybody."

It almost came to blows. The group broke up and I started walking away.

The guy from my squad came up to me. "Danny, could you imagine that Jamaican motherfucker thinking that he was better than us? I should have punched that nigger right in the face. Come on, let's go have a beer!"

The whole situation was interesting. It gave me a little different outlook on the black society. The black power brothers united genre of the sixties was not necessarily reflective of the black society, especially the soldiers in Vietnam. Most of them were nominally for it, some could care less but to the infantry black soldier it was irrelevant. They knew like we knew that it was not germaine to our situation, staying alive was germaine.

I did hear of some talk of a black power movement among some troops in the rear but I never experienced it first hand and I do not really know if there was any substance to it. There were always rumors in the army.

I did however, experience black bigotry. One day while we were in the rear a couple of us stopped by one of the artillery bunkers. There were some people from the second platoon, from the artillery, and again I was the only white person there. After a while a discussion broke out that I was not part of. One of the guys from the second platoon, he was from Chicago, was saying that he did not like white boys and began to expound. One of the guys from my squad interrupted, "Hey, 'red' is over here." The guy looked at me. He was startled and did not realize that I was there. "Hey, red's all right. I did not mean you, but I really do not like most white boys."

There was some mumbling of agreement in the background. I stood up, we glared at each other. He said, "Hey, we're friends, do not take me wrong. Just like there are whites that don't like blacks, there are blacks that do not like whites. Sorry man."

We went through one of those black handshakes and we both sat down. I left shortly thereafter. I am pretty thick skinned and it did not really bother me but it did affect me. From that day on I became aware not to be the only white among blacks. I spent a lot of my free time with the whites anyway. Not because of race but it just seemed to work out that way. Prior to this happening, there was an incident with one of the white southerners. One day he said something to the effect as to why was I hanging out with those colored boys. I yelled back at him, "What the fuck is it your business where I spend my time?" I was pissed. I started walking towards him. A bunch of the good old boys jumped up and said, "Why are you picking on 'red'? He's a good old boy. It's just that he is from New York. They're different up there." Nothing else was said.

I basically got along with everybody and as I said, race was not a major factor. There was one day when it even helped me out. We were back in the rear and we were on stand down, that is, three days of doing absolutely nothing, sort of like a rest. It was a very secure area. One of the places where the cherries came after they were assigned to a unit but before they actually joined their unit.

I was walking across the compound, I had just finished mailing some letters. I was in country about seven months at the time and we had just come in off the field. The respite was welcome. While walking across the compound I noticed a couple of people waiting on line at the mess tent. Normally I would never wait on a line that I did not have to, but a hot meal was inviting. It would hit the spot. I was about third or fourth in line and was there about ten minutes. The line grew substantially. The next thing, a black mess sergeant, an E7, came out, pointed to the first six or seven in line and said, "Your serving the meal." I walked over to the sergeant and said, "Hey sarge, I just came in from the field, why don't you get one of the cherries to serve. I just want to eat."

I really expected him to honor my request. It was a traditional job for a cherry to serve.

"I told you to get in there and serve, now get in there."

"There is no way I am going to serve a bunch of cherries."

He got mad. "Boy, I told you to….."

"Boy? Who are you calling boy? (I got that from the blacks) Take your meal and shove it."

I started to walk away. He kept shouting then he grabbed my arm. It might have looked like I punched him but I did not. I just threw him off of me with a forward motion of my arm. He was not a big man. He went reeling back about eight or ten feet and fell to the ground. He started to get up. I was ranting and raving. "You rear echelon, cock sucking bastard, who the fuck do you think you are? Put your hands on me? Don't come any closer, I will fucking kill you."

He stayed his distance. "Come on into the kitchen and we'll settle this."

"Fuck you. You wanna settle this, let's go right here." I was like a mad man. I started to go towards him. He quickly started walking away.

"Come on into the kitchen."

I was yelling and screaming. He went into the kitchen and I started to follow but then I thought twice. What was I going to do, go in there and get stabbed by eighty-six cooks? I went back to my tent.

About a half-hour later, in came a lieutenant.

"Coughlin, did you punch the mess sergeant?"

"No sir."

"Did you call him a nigger?"

"No sir."

Not that at the time I wouldn't have called him all the niggers in the world but it basically was not a part of my vocabulary.

"What happened?"

I explained exactly what happened including the expletives, there was an old time white sergeant there. "Hey lieutenant, you know how they are, you give them a little authority and it goes right to their heads."

The lieutenant seemed to listen.

"Coughlin, the sergeant wants to have you court martialed."

I looked at him and shrugged my shoulders. Although I did not want a court martial, we both knew it would get me out of the field.

"He wants an apology."

"No way sir. He should be court martialed, he attacked me."

"You disobeyed a direct order."

"That was chicken shit."

"Sit down and be quiet, I'll get back to you."

About two hours later the captain came walking into the tent. He had me standing at attention and was reading the riot act to me. I just kept saying, "Yes sir. No sir. Thank you sir." But by now it was apparent that nothing was going to happen to me. The captain said that he had interceded upon my behalf. After all this man was not part of the 82nd and from what some of the witnesses said he wasn't exactly telling the truth.

"I talked him into dropping all the charges but you will have to apologize."

"No sir." I explained that I was not going to apologize to him that I would rather be court martialed.

"You mean you would rather be court martialed than to apologize to the sergeant?"

"I wouldn't apologize to that man."

I meant it personal but I think the captain took it as racial, he was a southerner.

"You are confined to quarters."

He left. About a half hour later the captain came back, he did not seem angry.

"I just saved your ass. There will be no court martial and you will not have to apologize. The 82nd takes care of its own. You will be confined to quarters until we leave here."

"Yes sir. Thank you sir."

"Do you have any questions?"

"Yes sir." With a half smile on my face, I asked him if I was allowed to go and eat. He looked at me but he could not help but to smile. He shook his head as he left the tent.

"You're confined to quarters."

Now I really don't know if that meant if I was forbidden to eat for three days but there was no way I would go near that mess tent. The sergeant would probably poison me. I am sure he was pissed. Besides C-Rations really weren't that bad. You got used to them.

I am not saying that I did not get off because the 82nd takes care of its own because they did. The fact that I was white and the lieutenant, the captain, and the major, were also white might have had something to do with it. If it were a white mess sergeant I would have acted the same. Would the army's decision have been the same? I tend to doubt it but then again, if it had been a white mess sergeant he never would have made me serve the meal.

The military as an institution had a history of race bias just like many other institutions in America had. By the time I entered the military they were doing their best to end these practices and were fairly successful at it but I am sure some latent forms of racism did exist.

The awarding of medals in Vietnam was a very strange process. Some instances the process was automatic. For example, if you were in the infantry and you spent five months on line you would be awarded an army accommodation medal. If you spent seven months on line, you would be awarded the Bronze Star. The army also has a Bronze Star with a "V". The "V" standing for valor. This was supposed to be awarded for bravery in the field. This was not always the case. Sometimes they would allocate a certain amount of medals to a unit. The unit would arbitrarily award them to the people they chose.

Most of the time, you would have to be recommended for a medal because of some feat of bravery. The recommendation almost always came through. This is where the process became sticky. Who was doing the recommendations? Who were they recommending? What was the criteria for these recommendations? This process did not always seem fair and at times was completely out of line. The sergeant who was telling the story about walking into the N.V.A. point man and was removed from the field because of his in actions on ambush. In the interim he was awarded a Bronze Star with a "V". He was recommended because some officer liked the way he walked point. Hard to believe, but he is a decorated hero.

There was a lieutenant who was with us who received two Silver Stars. Probably deserved both. He was a brave man and a good leader. He received one Silver Star because the enemy threw a grenade into his position, he picked it up and threw it out before it exploded, saving many lives. I do not recall the other instance.

There were many other instances where people did things and were not rewarded. One in particular, a black sergeant, Sergeant Hodges (real name) went above and beyond the call of duty and was not rewarded. We were ambushed and the enemy was firing at us. One of the fairly new sergeants to the field stood up and ran towards the enemy. He motioned for others to follow. Sergeant Hodges yelled for them to get down but too much was going on. They ran across a booby trapped area. There were explosions, people were down. Sergeant Hodges ran to their rescue. He knew he was going across the booby trapped area, in fact, he tripped one but he was moving so fast that he was not hit. The enemy was still firing. We were returning fire but it was tricky. Our own men were in front of us.

The new sergeant had made a mistake. It cost him his life. Sergeant Hodges tried to rectify it. He put his own life in extreme danger to help the other men. He took charge. The enemy retreated. It was a very brave thing. No medal was awarded.

Why? It is hard to say. Basically, no one put him in for one. Was he not put in for a medal because he was black? No. That wouldn't be a factor, at least not directly. Let's look at the situations.

The lieutenant was a white career soldier, a West Point graduate. I am sure that two Silver Stars helped his career immensely. He deserved them but why was he put in for them? Being an officer, did he talk to the captain and ask for the recommendation? Probably. Nothing wrong with that if you deserve it. Was there a little bit of the good old boy syndrome here? Probably. There were a lot of politics involved with the awarding of medals.

Did the sergeant deserve a medal? Definitely. In my opinion at least a Silver Star. Why wasn't he put in for one? He was not part of that good old boy network. He was a career soldier, and E7. I am sure a medal would have enhanced his career. He was a good soldier but he was not a kiss ass. Nobody thought to go out of their way in recommending him for a medal. He did not know enough about the politics of the situation to push for it himself or he did not want to toot his own horn. Somehow he was overlooked.

If he were a white sergeant in the same situation, would he have been put in for a medal? I would have bet on it. One of the mechanisms would have kicked in. Was Sergeant Hodges denied a medal because he was black? No, but did the fact that he was black have anything to do with the outcome? A strong case could be made for it but then again some people got medals they did not deserve and some did not get medals that they did deserve. Race might not have been a factor.

The bottom line is that Sergeant Hodges was an American soldier who deserved recognition that he did not receive for whatever reason.

Sometimes it is hard to judge what is racial and what is not racial but race to one degree or another was part of the Vietnam experience.

Drugs

One of the biggest misconceptions of the Vietnam War was that the soldiers in the field were constantly high on drugs. This simply was not true.

Drugs did exist, especially marijuana, and at one time or another most Vietnam Veterans did smoke pot but the use of pot was not universal and for the infantry soldier, had its time and place. Drugs were more readily available in some areas than others.

The first time I smoked pot in Vietnam, I had to be in country at least three months. We were sent out in the field. Pot was simply not readily available to us.

We were back in a rear area base camp and one of the guys on garbage detail bought some pre-rolled joints from one of the Vietnamese. That evening a bunch of us gathered around and we smoked the joints. It was a novelty. First time for most of us, even the guys who had been in country since Tet. It was fun. The officers knew what was going on but it did not seem to bother them.

We were in the rear three or four days and since we now knew where to buy pot, someone would buy it and we would smoke it. Smoking pot got you high. It was a nice feeling. Some people got silly, some people got sleepy, we all got hungry. We were in the rear, it did not seem to matter and it did relieve stress. You became relaxed.

Then the party was over and we went back in the field. To this point in time no one had ever smoked pot in the field. The first couple of nights out a few of the guys smoked pot. It started to upset a lot of people. First the smell of pot was very distinctive, if the enemy was in the area, they would know that you were around just from the smell.

Next thing, people tended to get sleepy. You were tired enough to begin with, no one wanted anyone falling asleep while on guard. Then there was the fact that you depended on the people you were with to stay alive. No one wanted anyone stoned out of their face when you might have to depend on their reactions for your survival. We had a meeting among the guys and we decided that no one was to smoke pot while we were out in the field. A few people did not see the problem but they were let known that this was now a fact of life. No smoking in the field. It was relegated just for the rear areas. The whole time we were up north no one smoked pot in the field again, at least not to my knowledge.

Down south was a whole different story, pot was plentiful. You seemed to be able to get it at anytime. It was much more abused.

During the transition from up north to down south they had us in a rear area base camp for about three weeks with almost nothing to do. The smoking of pot became a regular activity. Daytime, nighttime, just about any time, people were getting high. It seemed that in the rear people smoked a lot of pot. I am sure there were people who smoked pot everyday that they were in Vietnam. It became a part of their existence, something to do or something to escape to. If you were not involved with combat Vietnam could become very boring. Smoking pot would pass the time. There were a lot of people who just liked it.

Then the time came when we were sent back out into the field. Again, pot smoking was regulated to the rear areas, at least in the beginning. They had us in this area west of Saigon for two to three months. There was no enemy in the area. We went on patrols, set ambushes, searched villages, but there was nothing there. Slowly people started smoking pot out in the field. Then it became a regular activity. Nobody seemed to complain because for all intents and purposes there was no war going on around us. For a while all we did was string barbed wire around villages, go on meaningless patrols and pull ambushes that never materialized. Now you would think that everyone would be happy that we weren't really involved in combat. We were but it was frustrating. You wondered what the hell you were doing there. Pot became a natural outlet.

Later on when we were back involved in the war, I remember thinking how nice it would be just to sit around those villages and smoke pot all day.

When we were back in combat situations, again, nobody smoked pot in the field. There were some fire bases that were as bad as being in the field. Pot was not smoked there either. Nobody had to tell anybody, you just knew. It became an unwritten law. Most of us were in country seven, eight months or better, smoking pot in the field or in troubled areas was not part of your road to survival. We were now short timers and staying alive became very real again.

Although it was the most frequently used, pot was not the only drug used in Vietnam. For a short while speed was being used. Speed was an altogether different drug. It was an upper. It would give you energy. You could stay up for twenty four hours straight without being tired or hungry. At first, it seemed like an excellent drug for pulling guard all night in bad areas but then we discovered the side effects. When the drug wore off you crashed. You felt terrible. You needed sleep, but the sleep you got was not restful. Speed soon vanished from the field, not because it was not available but because it really did not do us any good out there. You just could not perform the duties you had to while coming down from this drug. The drug remained quite popular for some people in the rear. I do not know how many people became addicted to it but there were a lot of people in the rear using it.

When I got back to the world I heard a lot of talk about the use of heroin in Vietnam. The whole time I was there, I never saw any heroin or knew anyone who did heroin. I am not saying that the drug was never there, but I never ran across it. What I did experience there was opium and heroin is a derivative of opium.

Opium is a very strange drug. I tried it on two occasions, it was a unique experience. One day I was in the rear base camp at Ton-Son-Nut. One of the guys in the rear said, come on let's go into Saigon. We didn't have passes but he showed me how to get in anyway. Right outside the gate across the street, upstairs in one of the buildings was an opium den. I didn't know that's where we were going but once I realized it I figured, what the hell? I will try anything once. Vietnam helped foster that attitude.

When we got inside there were seven or eight GI's just sitting there. They were really stoned. There were two old Vietnamese men who also looked pretty stoned, they ran the place. The guy I was with went first. He had about ten hits. They charged fifty cents a hit. Then it was my turn, I sat in a chair and one old man was holding a pipe. The pipe must have been four feet long. On the other end of the pipe was the other old man. He was rolling the opium into a small ball, it looked like a putty type substance. He put it into the bowl at the end of the pipe and lit it. I was told to draw in on the pipe for as long as I could. It was different than smoking pot or even a cigarette which you drew the smoke in for a few seconds. The opium you would draw in for as long as you could. Twenty, thirty seconds or more. The first time I choked. The old men were laughing calling me a cherry boy. They knew it was the first time I had tried it. I had seven or eight hits. I felt it right away. It was a unique sensation. You got very stoned. Everything was in slow motion. Periodically, your blood felt like it was rushing to your head, you became more stoned, barely able to move. Somehow we made it back to camp, I was still very stoned, the rushes kept coming. They felt good but made me a little dizzy. At one point I got sick, but even getting sick was different. I threw up and being sick was over. I just sat there in this euphoric state of slow motionless. Finally I went to sleep.

I went one other time with the same guy but I really do not know why, this was not for me. I realized the other guy was addicted. There were probably a lot of people who became addicted to opium but at the time I am sure few people realized that they were addicted.

Morphine was also readily available from the medics. I am sure that there were people who became addicted to morphine either through legitimate use or abuse but I never knew anyone in our unit to abuse morphine.

Most of us in Vietnam did not realize the potential dangers inherent in drugs. It was immediate gratification and few people cared about long term effects. There were more immediate dangers on your mind than the long term effects of drugs. Once in a while the short term effects can be very dangerous.

We were back in a rear area fire base, I was in country about seven or eight months at the time. The fire base was in a fairly safe area. We had been to this base four or five times before, nothing really going on there. One evening we had a marathon pot smoking session. It must have lasted two or three hours. Every time you turned around someone else was handing you a bowl. It got ridiculous. You could not smoke anymore when someone else was handing you some more. Finally it broke up. I was walking back to my bunker. I was very stoned and a little dizzy. I remember thinking that I was glad that I did not have to pull guard that night. I got to the bunker and climbed on top. There was a full moon that night. I was just lying there looking up at the sky, the moon was reflecting off of the clouds. The clouds were appearing as different objects, I guess I was hallucinating. It was very peaceful. All of a sudden there was an explosion then another. We were being mortared. They were landing about one hundred yards away on the other side of the base. I started to get up but I could not move. Every time I would lift my head up I became so dizzy that the only thing I could do was put my head down again. Boom! Another explosion. A fear came over me. What the hell was I going to do? Don't panic. If I just lie here it would probably take a direct hit to get me and if there was a direct hit I probably would not be much safer inside the bunker. Boom! A little closer. What if the mortars were a diversion and Charlie was going to attack this side of the compound. I just cannot lie here. I lifted my head. The whole compound was spinning. I put it down again. I felt helpless. Boom! I got to do something! My weapon was in my hand. I reached for my ammo and rolled off the bunker. It was about a five foot fall, it gave me a jolt, nothing serious. My head began to clear. I went into the bunker and looked out to see if we were being attacked. The mortaring continued for another couple of minutes and then it was over.

From the time that the first mortar hit until I rolled off the bunker, maybe thirty seconds had passed. Not a long time but that thirty seconds could have ended my life. I never participated in a marathon pot smoking session again.

That was the only time pot had affected me in a combat situation but there were some non-combat situations where pot had a negative influence.

It was the first time that I was back in the rear at Ton Son Nut. I came in from the field to go to the dentist because I had some teeth knocked out when were up north. A strange occurrence. We were on a fire base in a bad area. We were all in a central location getting the poop on what was going on the next day. Somebody shot up a red flare. A red flare signified that you were under attack. We were all running to our positions. My bunker was actually outside the perimeter. As I was running towards the bunker, people started shooting. I dove to the ground. My face hit something. A little blood, but I wasn't really hurt, I was concerned about being attacked. It turned out to be a false alarm. The next day one of my teeth came out. Now it was about two months later and the one next to it was bothering me. That is what I was doing back in the rear.

That night a couple of us were smoking pot and talking about going into Saigon the next day. We were drinking beer and smoking pot and we were very hungry. There was nothing to eat. One of the guys thought that I had gotten a package sent to me that day and it was still in the rear. I knew that if my mother had sent a package that there would be food. We went to look. There it was. I opened the package. And inside among other things, was this large can of ham. It was the type that had the key you used to open it. You had to put the piece of metal into the hole in the key and keep turning until it opened. I was a little stoned.

The key broke off about half way around. I tried pulling it open. My hand slipped and the palm of my hand went right into the razor sharp edge of the can. I looked at it. I was bleeding and the cut was pretty deep. I put pressure on it, held my hand above my heart, and went to the battalion aid station. When we arrived there was no doctor just a P.F.C. medic. He looked at my hand and said that it was going to need stitches. He got the equipment and was about to start stitching when he turned to this other P.F.C. medic and asked if he had ever seen this done before. I pulled my hand away.

"What do you mean, have you ever seen this done before? You never did this?"

He laughed and assured me that he had done this many times. He just wanted to know if the other guy had ever done it before. I was a little skeptical. If he was so experienced, why was he still a P.F.C.? I didn't have much of a choice. I let him stitch my hand.

When it was over, we went back to our area, opened the can, washed off the blood, and ate the ham.

Looking at my hand now, the guy did a very good job. He put in about eight stitches and you can hardly see the scar. Actually cutting my hand turned out to be a pretty good thing. The medic put a large bandage on my hand. It kept me in the rear for a while and I got to go into Saigon regularly.

While I was still in the rear, one of the guys from my platoon came back. He was on his way to Hawaii for R&R. He was going to meet his fiancee and officially become engaged. The next day he was going into Saigon to buy her an engagement ring. I had an appointment at the hospital in Saigon. He met me there. Then we went off to buy the ring. We went to this gigantic P.X. in Saigon. They had everything. He bought this beautiful ring, then we went out on the town.

Saigon was a very exciting place. Although there were no tall buildings and was primitive by modern standards, still it had the feel of the big city. The hustle and bustle, plenty of bars and restaurants. We started walking the streets going from one bar to another. Then we came across a pharmacy. My partner started talking to them about buying drugs. It seemed that they would sell, what would be in the states prescription drugs, right over the counter. He bought something called binactals. They were a barbiturate, a downer. We popped a couple and continued to bar hop. It was getting late, we were pretty stoned. We decided to stay in Saigon for the night. They had a curfew there. You had to be off the streets by 10:00 P.M. We each got on the back of a motorcycle, they were unauthorized taxi cabs. We told them to take us to Tudor street. That was a place where they had plenty of bars and rooms that you could rent for the night.

When we arrived I paid my driver, turned around and my partner was arguing with his driver. He thought the driver was charging him too much. I told him to pay the guy and let's get out of here, but there was no talking to him. If you ever saw a person stoned on downs, you know that they can become very belligerent. He was really stoned. He must have taken more than me.

The next thing the MP's were there, they separated us. We did not have overnight passes. I was explaining to this one MP, how I got wounded in the field and was in Saigon to go to the hospital, that my partner was on his way for R&R and we were just having a few drinks to celebrate. He bought my story and was about to let me go. Then I heard my partner yelling at the MP's. They had handcuffed him and were roughing him up. I started to go over. The one MP grabbed my arm.

"If you go over there, we are going to lock you up."

I thought for a second and then they smashed my partner's face into the hood of the jeep. I ran over yelling, "What is wrong with you guys? We're out in the field risking our lives and this is how we get treated when we get back to the rear?"

They turned around and saw the bandage on my hand. They stopped beating on my partner but locked us both up. They kept us overnight then turned us over to the 82nd MP's. They brought us back to our unit. Then we had to face top. Top is the nickname for the first sergeant in charge of the company. Top was an ornery old guy from Wyoming. He did not particularly like New Yorkers. We went into his tent. He started yelling, "What's wrong with you guys? What the hell were you doing in Saigon fighting with MP's? Wait till I get done with you…."

My partner spoke up, "Top, it was not our fault."

"Don't tell me that, what happened?"

My partner started giving him a story, "Remember you said we could go into Saigon to buy an engagement ring. Well we bought the ring and we started walking through Saigon. The MP's stopped us and started harassing us. Who do you guys from the 82nd think you are? Every time you come in here, you are out of uniform. What do you think you are a bunch of tough guys who can do what they want. There are regulations and you guys from the 82nd are going to start adhering to them. Then he pushed me. What could I do? I took a swing at him. They jumped all over me. Danny came to help. We both wound up being locked up. Top, they should not be allowed…"

"Is that how your face got like that?"

His face was all messed up. Top looked at me. "Is that what happened?"

"That is exactly the way it happened."

He looked at us, not sure whether to believe us or not. He paused a moment, "Where is the engagement ring?"

My partner produced the ring. It was like that was all the proof needed to believe us. "You guys get out of here."

As we are leaving the tent you could hear top yelling, "This is not the first time the MP's messed with the 82nd." He was going to put a stop to this. "Get the MP's on the horn!"

It seems the 82nd does take care of its own.

Meanwhile, we were very lucky. My partner left for R&R. Top was going to send me out to the field but I still had a bandage on my hand. He sent me out to a fire base. He said he wanted me out of his hair. I was happy to go.

When I got out to the fire base, my platoon was there. The lieutenant asked me what happened. I told him I cut it and the stitches were supposed to come out in two days. He said that we were going out to the field next day and asked if I was all right to go. I said that someone had to take the stitches out. He said that the medic could do it and that he was short of men. I could have refused, but I figured I was pretty lucky with the MP situation and I could use a few brownie points. I told him I would go. He asked if I would take the point. My hand was all right, the bandage was only there to keep it clean. I took the point.

The next morning we were moving out, I was on point. We were just leaving the fire base when a jeep was pulling in. The jeep stopped. It was the captain who was our commander up north. He called me over.

"I see you were wounded. Are you all right?"

"Yes sir."

"It does my heart good to see a wounded soldier with the guts and desire to walk point."

Then he did something that was very unusual for a field officer. He gave me a salute. In order not to identify who the officers were in a field unit, the practice of saluting was not adhered to in the field. He said, "Airborne."

I responded with, "All the way sir."

He smiled and his jeep took off.

I was sort of laughing to myself. I wondered what he would have thought if he knew that I was stoned out of my face and cut my hand on a can of ham? Well, he wouldn't have been proud but then again, he would not have cared that I was stoned either. There lies one of the biggest problems in Vietnam. Nobody cared. You would think that the use of drugs would be abhorrent to the military that they would do everything within their power to stop the use of drugs. They didn't. The whole time I was in Vietnam I never saw anyone busted for using drugs. Not even an article 15. There were rumors that they were going to have crack downs but basically the military seemed to have a hands off approach. I am not saying that you would walk in to talk to a colonel with a joint in your hand but if you did not bother them they did not bother you.

The only time I ever saw them getting involved was one time they sent a directive down to the medics that they had to account for their use of morphine. I do not know if that was to combat the abuse of morphine or they simply had a supply problem.

Everyone knew that the use of drugs was illegal but that seemed to be only a technicality. Like betting on a football pool. Everyone knows that they are illegal, but no one cares. There is not a bar in New York that does not run a Super Bowl pool. Every office has someone who sells football tickets. Even the police bet a couple of dollars on the football pools. You can't read the sports section without seeing a betting line. Is betting legal? No. Does anybody care about the small time football pools? No. That's the way it was with drugs in Vietnam. It sent a very poor message to the troops. We are not telling you drugs are legal but if you use them there is nothing we are going to do about it unless you flaunt it to a point where you are going to force us to act. This "laissez-faire" approach to drugs seemed to be the accepted U.S. policy toward drugs in Vietnam.

When the veterans returned home to the states the military and civilian policy towards drugs was different. The Veteran had to adjust but might not have seen the need or have the will to do so. This was only one of many adjustments that caused potential problems for the returning Veteran.

Sex

Since the beginning of war itself, sex has played an intricate part in the life of a soldier. Vietnam was no exception.

Sex like drugs was either very plentiful or very sparse, depending on where you were in country. The whole time we spent up north I did not have a sexual experience nor did I have the opportunity. If I had been able to spend time in Hue or Da Nang it would have been different. Unfortunately, anytime that I spent there it was on military time not leisure time.

There was also a place up north for in country R&R. I believe it was China Beach. I heard that sex was plentiful but I did not get the opportunity. The rumor had it that the North Vietnamese army also took their R&R in the same area. I found that hard to believe but that is what we were told.

Down south was a whole other world. Sex was all around you. The first time that I had the opportunity was the time I got arrested. Unfortunately, the MP's arrived before I got to go in.

My first experience there really was not very thrilling. It happened one day when we were out in the field. Two whores came out and we all lined up, for a small price, we each took a turn. It was something that I participated in only that one time. There was something unappealing about being eighth or tenth or fifteenth on line, laying down with this woman, having an orgasm and then letting the next guy go. Periodically the whores came out to the field but it was not for me.

Then I discovered Saigon. What a great place Saigon was for someone who was a combat soldier or for that matter for any single male. Women were everywhere. In the brothels, in the bars, in the hotels, they just inundated the city. They were prostitutes but not like prostitutes that you would find in the States. Once you paid the money they no longer seemed like prostitutes. Once money exchanged hands these women became your lover, your companion, your friend, just someone who was very nice to spend time with. I never had a bad experience with a woman in Saigon and I am sure that was true for most soldiers.

I technically used to go AWOL anytime I got the opportunity to get into Saigon. I would stay until my money ran out and then go back to my unit. They would yell a little but they knew the story. There was not much worse that they could do to you but send you back out to the field. As long as it was only for a day or two, they left you alone. The 82nd rarely gave you a pass to go into Saigon and if they did they wanted you to go to one specific brothel. That was because they sent a doctor out there each week to check the women in order to prevent the spread of disease. This was either a very innovative medical policy or the kick backs were good from this brothel.

A typical jaunt into Saigon usually went like this: you were back in the rear, but they would not give you a pass. So you would catch a ride to the Vietnamese Officers Club. The officer's club, which would let in any American soldier, was right on the border of Ton Son Nut and Saigon. The club was a typical sex haunt. There was a large bar and many tables. The club was filled with bar girls. You would have a drink and buy a girl a Saigon tea. Saigon tea was supposedly vodka but there really was no liquor in it. For the privilege of buying a tea, you could have a conversation in broken English and maybe a little kissing and feeling of each other. Then you would have another drink and more of the same. You could stay there and get a room with the girls but it was very expensive. I would usually stay for a drink or two and then off to Saigon. There were only two gates that led into Saigon. One was controlled by the Americans, the other by the Vietnamese. If you went to the officer's club, you could catch a ride with the Vietnamese through their gate and into Saigon. They would take you to a brothel. You would pay them for the ride and then off you were.

Once you got inside the brothel you were greeted by a host. She would bring you into a room and show you all the ladies that were available. You would choose a woman and pay the host. Usually, twenty dollars or less for the girl and the room for the night. The girl was there to please you. Whatever you wanted to do, the girls were willing. If you wanted a massage, then sex, or sex first, then a massage, if you wanted to talk or kiss or have sex all night long, the girls were not only willing they also seemed to enjoy it. Sometimes you would be with them into the next morning. It was past your time and the mamasons wanted you out of there but the girls seemed to like having you around. Sometimes I would spend the better part of the day with them, talking and laughing and hiding from the mamasons. The whole thing was usually a very pleasurable experience.

After one such jaunt into Saigon I returned to the rear then they sent me out to my unit. My company had just come in from the field to guard a bridge. This was more like a rest because the Vietnamese secured the bridge. Across from the bridge, there were three houses of ill repute.

The company had just gotten back and everyone was anxious to get to one of the houses. They needed someone for radio watch. I had just come back from a couple of days in Saigon plus I had no money, so I volunteered. There were a couple of guys hanging around so we started playing cards while monitoring the radio. After a couple of hours a call came for the sergeant, he was not around. They said that it was important and to have him call back as soon as possible. I had someone watch the radio and I went to one of the houses to look for him. I asked if anyone had seen Sergeant Stone.

"Yeah, he's inside with one of the women."

I did not want to disturb him, so I figured that I would wait. This Vietnamese woman came walking towards me and asked if she could help me. I explained that I was waiting for the sergeant. We started talking. She spoke perfect English. I was looking at her, she was beautiful, smooth skin, sparkling eyes, sensuous lips. There was an automatic chemistry between us, it became overpowering. We started to kiss. Her lips were warm and soft, our tongues touched ever so lightly, they seemed to melt together, her body came close to mine. We kissed for a long time. Then we separated, I looked at her, she seemed even more beautiful. The guys were yelling things at me but I paid no attention. I was floating on a cloud. She took my hand and I started to go with her. The sergeant was just coming out. I saw him and remembered what I was doing there and gave him the message. I explained to her that I had to go. She asked me to come back. I told her I would.

I went back to radio watch but I could not get her off my mind. She seemed so nice and beautiful and sensual. I just wanted her in my arms. It was all I could think about. Finally, I borrowed money, paid someone to take my watch, and went back to see her.

When I got back to the house, she was busy. They asked if I wanted another girl, I told them that I would wait. That I just wanted to see her. (As much as I am searching my mind, I cannot remember her name, I can picture what she looks like, but her name escapes me.) Then she came out. She smiled and took me by the hand and we went into a room. We talked for a while, kissed for a while, made love for a while. Then she explained that she was not on her own time and asked if I could come back later and spend the night. I told her that I was not sure but I would try.

I was on radio watch, I did not have to pull guard that night. Guard was sort of secondary anyway because the Vietnamese were in charge of the area. Now the only problem that remained was that the houses were off limits at night but I was not going to let that stop me. Besides, I was told that some of the officers went over there at night.

Just before dark I went over to the house. I told the guys in my squad where I would be, just in case. When I got there she was waiting for me. She was all dressed up. She had make up on. She looked absolutely gorgeous. I was spellbound.

We started talking and kissing. I was on cloud nine. She told me to take my clothes off and lie down and she would give me a massage. Her hands felt so good. She massaged every muscle in my body. By now I was lying on my back. She told me to lie there. She started to remove her clothes. She did it slowly and sensually. It was beautiful. We started to kiss. We explored each other's bodies kissing and touching for the longest time. She was ever so tender. Then our bodies joined together. We moved together ever so slowly until we worked into a pace that brought me to a state of near ecstasy. We both became satisfied and slowly calmed down then we continued the sequence once again. Our bodies were in harmony then we came to rest.

She lay down next to me. She asked if I was all right. I just smiled. She said that she never felt such sensations in her life. I do not know if she was saying that to make me feel good or if it was true. At the time it did not matter. I felt great. Then we got up and she sat me down on this bench. She drew water from a well and started washing me. It felt good. She gave me a towel to dry off. Then she asked if I was hungry. She left and came back in about ten minutes with some food. The problem was that the only utensils were chopsticks. I never used them before. She started to teach me. I was a little clumsy at first but I got the hang of it. We were laughing. Then this mamason came in and started yelling at her in Vietnamese. They went off to the side and they started yelling at each other. I thought it would come to blows. Then she came back and said she was sorry. She told the mamason that I was her guest but she insisted on getting paid. I told her, no problem and asked how much she wanted. She apologized and explained that she did not want any money but the mamason insisted on getting something. She asked for three dollars. I gave it to her and she gave it to the mamason. We continued to eat. Then we just talked and laughed. It was a pleasure to talk to a woman who understood what you said and did not talk back to you in broken English. She spoke English fluently. She was a very bright lady. We went back to bed, made love and went to sleep.

Then the morning came, we got up, we talked a little bit, I had to go. She asked if I could come back that night. I told her I would be there. I went back to my company and took radio watch all day, so I would not have to pull guard that night. That night came, the same thing. I could not get enough of her, I liked being with her. I liked talking to her and the lovemaking was fabulous. That night we talked for a long time without even an interruption from the mamason. She told me that she was living with an Air Force Officer for a while and that he had promised to marry her and bring her to America. Then his tour was over and he went home. She asked me if I thought he would ever come back. I told her no. She looked sad, I felt bad for her. Then she smiled and said that she knew that he would not come back but she wished she could go to America because there was no life left for her in Vietnam. We talked some more. She told me that she did not want to be a whore but there were no other options left for her. Then she told me how strange it was that we were together. She promised herself that she would not get emotionally involved again unless she was to get married and change her life, yet here she was with me. She knew that I would be gone but she thought she was falling in love with me. Then she asked me if I was falling in love with her. At first, I did not know what to say, because if this was not love that I was feeling then I did not know what it was. I told her that I thought I was but I also told her that we would never be together because the war and life was going to take us in different directions. She said she knew that but she was happy I felt the way I did. We talked some more then we lay down, made love and went to sleep.

Morning came but I did not want to leave. I told her I was falling in love with her but something to the effect that war was hell and I had to go. She asked if I could come back that night. I told her yes. Unfortunately, that day we pulled out.

About a week later we were on a squad sized patrol near the area. I took the patrol over to the bridge. There was not much time. We met and talked for about ten minutes and then we kissed good-bye. I told her I would be back but we left that area of Vietnam altogether. I never saw her again.

There were not many chances for a field soldier to have a relationship with a woman. You were always on the go. For the people who lived in the rear it was a different story. A lot of people who were housed in the rear had girls who came in to clean, do laundry or whatever. I am sure many relationships were formed. For the field soldier it was more like wham bam thank you Ma'am. For most of us you had sex whenever you could. You lived under the guise of eat, drink, and be merry for tomorrow you may die.

The military also played a role. They allowed sex to become available by bringing you back to areas that had whore houses or by sending you on R&R.

You had your pick of where you wanted to go on R&R, such as Bangkok, Singapore, Malaysia, Hong Kong, Australia, Hawaii, just to name a few. I chose Australia for my first R&R. I was in country ten months before I went. That was by my own design. Most people took R&R when they were in country about six months. R&R meant that you were out of the field for about two weeks. Three days going, three days coming back and seven days there. I stretched it out a couple of days longer. When I got back to the rear, the first thing I did was go to Saigon for a couple of nights. Then it was off to Australia.

Upon landing in Australia, they gave you specific instructions. Such as: do not over tip. Only tip the cab driver to the nearest dime. If the ride is sixty nine cents, you give him seventy. They did not want the Americans messing up the Australian way of life. They made it perfectly clear that if you got into any trouble whatsoever, you would be sent back to Vietnam immediately.

They landed us in country about ten in the morning. I buddied up with a guy from the 82nd, 2/505. After we got settled in our rooms at Bondi Beach, just outside of Sydney. We were off to Sydney. There was not much to do so we started to drink. We drank all day and into the night. That became a little tricky because they close the pubs at certain hours and you had to drink in the hotels. Then the pubs reopened. We wound up at a place at King's Cross called Whiskey A Go-Go. It was a bar discotheque. It was a nice place. We were drinking and laughing and talking to a few girls, then I do not remember what happened. The next thing I knew I woke up and it was completely dark. I grabbed for my weapon, it was not there. I did not know where I was. It took a few seconds then I realized that I was in the john. I had fallen asleep on the bowl. I felt my way through the dark and found the door. I went into the bar area. There was no one there, the bar was closed, everyone had left. Now, leaving an Irishman in a bar all alone was like leaving a kid alone in a candy store. I had a drink, then another, then I thought that they might be thinking that I was robbing the place, and send me back to Vietnam. What was I going to do? I put money up on the bar. That way at least they could not accuse me of stealing the drinks. I had another. Then I went to the front door and looked outside. No one was there. It was just about day light. I tried the handle of the door and to my surprise the door opened. I went outside, closed the door, it locked. I got a cab and went back to the hotel.

The next day or really that day, we did a little sight seeing, went out to eat and back to the bars. We were in this one bar and we met a couple of girls. It was easy to talk to girls in Australia. They were plentiful plus it was a strange thing, the Australian men did not seem to bother with the women who were in the bars. They basically hung around with each other, drank beer, told stories, and pretty much left the women alone.

That night I left with one of the girls. She said she would come back to my hotel but she wanted to stop by her place first. I walked her there. She asked me to wait outside and she went in. A couple of minutes passed and I was about to leave, I figured she had dumped me. Then there she was. We went back to my hotel.

When we got into the room we started kissing and playing. Then we got into some heavy kissing. We stopped. I took my clothes off, we started kissing, I went to take her blouse off but she stopped me. I asked what was wrong. She said she had some female problems and she could not have sex. I did not know if I believed her. We started kissing again then I took her blouse off. I tired to take her pants off but she would not let me. I tried a couple of other times but she stopped me. I did not know if she wanted me to force her or rape her or what but I was only interested in a sexual relationship between two mutually consenting adults. I went to sleep. When I woke up in the morning she was still lying there next to me. I asked why she would not have sex with me. She told me that she originally was going to rob me, that when we stopped at her flat, a couple of her friends were going to mug me. I told her that she was lucky that they didn't, that I probably would have ended their lives. Then I asked her if she was going to rob me, why didn't she take my money while I was sleeping. She said that she was going to but she really did not know what to make of me. She said that she sort of liked me so she didn't. I did not know whether to believe her or what to make of her. Then there was a knock on my door. It was my buddy from the 2/505. I put my pants on and let him in. We all started talking for a while. Then she said she had to go. I gave her money for a cab and she left. My buddy was jealous. He was saying that he was going to get laid that night no matter what. I am in country two days and I haven't even been kissed and you are lying here with this woman. I was going to tell him that nothing happened but I do not think he would have believed me or maybe I didn't tell because of some sort of macho thing or a combination of both.

My friend saw the girl a couple of times after that. He kept telling me that she wanted to get together with me. I did not know what to make of this girl. I did not see her. A couple of days later I went out on a date with another woman but there was nothing more than a few kisses involved.

It was difficult, if not impossible to have a relationship, other than sexual, with a woman when you were thousands of miles from home and you knew you would see her for only a brief time during your journey.

When I got back to Vietnam, I went to Saigon, it was a pleasure to pay a couple of dollars and have fun for the night.

I also took a seven-day leave in Hong Kong. Hong Kong was a very exciting place. There, you bought a woman for a day, she became your companion, your lover, your guide. It was a very pleasant experience.

I guess you cannot write about sex without bringing up homosexuality but with the exception of two Vietnamese soldiers I saw grabbing each other one day I did not know of any other homosexuality that existed. I am sure it did, but I never saw it. The same thing with rape. I never knew or heard of any soldier who raped a Vietnamese woman. I am sure it went on but not in my unit.

I am not exactly sure how the sexual experience affected your attitude when you got back to the States but it would take a big adjustment just to go out on a date, hold hands and kiss goodnight.

While it may be said that the American GI's looked upon the Vietnamese woman merely as sex objects. This would not be totally true. They were more than just objects of sex. They were warm, kind, and caring women who fulfilled many needs in a very lonely and frightening place. They made the traumas of war a little bit easier to endure.

The People, The Environment, The Enemy

Vietnam was very different from twentieth century America. It was an anachronism. Like being placed in a time warp and returning to the seventeen hundreds or before.

The Vietnamese people led a very simple lifestyle. They lived in small villages consisting of grass roofed, mud walled, and dirt floored huts. There was no plumbing or electricity. They would draw their water from nearby wells, streams or rivers. There were no bathrooms or even outhouses. They would defecate in the rice paddies or fields outside of the villages.

They were basically an agricultural society whose main duties consisted of tending to the rice paddies or livestock around the village. I was never really sure if the rice paddies and livestock were owned individually by the people or collectively by the village.

Their usual day consisted of getting up at dawn, tending the fields till ten or eleven o'clock, when the sun became too hot, then returned to the village, eat and rest until late afternoon, back out to the fields till about an hour before dark. Then back to the village.

Some women would work the fields, others would stay home and cook and look out for the children. The old men, papasons, worked the fields and at night would drink their rice whiskey, smoke their homemade cigarettes and tell stories.

The most unusual thing was their eating habits. They would eat six to eight times a day. Mostly just rice with this horrible smelling sauce that they would put on top. If there was fish or game available they would cook it, chop it up and put it in the rice. I ate with the villagers a couple of times. The food smelled awful but it tasted pretty good.

One day we were on a break in this village. I was watching a couple of the kids about eight or nine years old playing by one of the wells. They would take a rock and tie it to this long rope like vine, throw it into the well then pull it up. They were doing this for about a half-hour when they got a little excited. One of the kids climbed into the well. He came up a couple of minutes later, he had a rat in his hand. They took it over to the mamason, she skinned it, put it on a stick, cooked it over an open fire. Then cut it into small pieces and put it in with the rice. Needless to say I stopped eating with the villagers.

The climate in Vietnam was either hot and dry or wet depending on the season. They had what you called monsoons. They were winds that when they came from the land would bring a dry climate that was very hot, although the constant breeze was somewhat refreshing. When the winds changed direction and came off the ocean, they would bring the rain. When they first started out they would bring rain at the same time everyday. Then the rains would come more often until it seemed like it was raining all the time. That led to a miserable existence. There were times when I was not dry for weeks, you walked in the rain, ate in the rain, slept in the rain, you were just constantly wet. This led to what we used to call jungle rot. These were sores that were all over your feet, sort of like athlete's foot but much, much worse. It looked like the skin was rotting from your body. You tried to keep your feet dry by taking off your boots and socks as much as possible. The army tried to keep you supplied with clean socks but you were just constantly wet. The sores got so bad on some people they could hardly walk. They were taken out of the field. Sores also appeared on other parts of the body but it was mainly the feet. The fact that you were wet all the time you would think that it would lead to other problems such as colds or respiratory infections but it didn't. I do not remember anyone having a cold. I know I didn't.

Aside from the constant rain they also had typhoons. One day we got caught in a typhoon that lasted for about four or five days. There was nothing that you could do. The storm was just too powerful. You just stayed in a makeshift tent that you made from your ponchos and tried to stay as dry as possible. After the third day a lot of us were running out of food. We couldn't get any supplies. We also ran out of heating tablets that were used to cook c-rations. They were small tablets that burned for eight to ten minutes. Very efficient but when we ran out people started using their claymore mines. Claymores were powered by C4, a plastic explosive. You could burn C4 without it exploding. It worked very well as a fuel. The army was not in love with us using their mines like that but under these conditions it was understandable. Now food was becoming really low. The rear said that they sent a chopper out, unusual in these weather conditions, but they could not locate us. They dropped the food anyway. One of the guys in my squad thought he heard something. He went out by himself and about fifteen minutes later, came back with a case of c-rations. He told the others where he found it. We divided the case and ate. I remember thinking that I was glad that they did not drop it on our heads.

As miserable of an existence as it was during the rainy season I do not remember ever having contact with the enemy.

When I got home, if I could help it, I would not go out in the rain. I would stay in the house, look at the rain and think how nice it was to be dry and comfortable when it was raining. My mother used to kid me and tell me that I would not melt if I went out in the rain. I just used to laugh to myself, I have been in rain. After a while I got over it. Now, sometimes I even like walking in it but I know it won't be long until I am dry and comfortable.

Rain was only one of the aspects of the environment that would mess with you. There were leeches, mosquitoes, ants, insects, snakes, and rats.

Leeches were the most unique. Most people when they think of leeches think of leeches that are in the water. They had them but they also had land leeches. They were found up north in the mountains. They were peculiar creatures. They were about two inches long and thinner than a cigarette. They would inch up on you. If they were climbing their head would stretch out and then the tail would come up to meet the head, the head would stretch out and the tail would come up to meet the head and so forth. If you did not feel them initially biting you, which most times you didn't, you wouldn't feel them until they filled up with blood and dropped off. When they bit you they would put an anti coagulant into you and the blood would flow into them. When they were twice the size and fatter than your finger they would fall off.

When you were in an area that had land leeches you were very careful. You made sure that you had as little skin exposed as possible. You would watch the back of the guy in front of you while also checking yourself. With all these precautions some still managed to get inside your clothes.

One day while on patrol in a leech infested area, I went to take a leak, I looked down and there was this leech full of blood right on the tip of my penis. "Hey look fellas, it grew." Everyone laughed. Then you had to remove it. The army developed a mosquito repellent that did not do much to repel mosquitoes, but a couple of drops on a leech they would pull out, fall off and die.

The leeches consumed a fair share of blood. I imagine enough of them could kill you. We were told about two marines, who were wounded, separated from their unit and died from exposure to leeches. I do not know if this was true but it was easy to believe. One night we had N.D.P. on this mountain top. The leeches came out in force. There were so many of them that they chased our whole company off of the mountain. The North Vietnamese never did that to us.

Then there were mosquitoes. In most areas they weren't that plentiful but in some areas they could drive you crazy. There were areas that were so infested that you could hardly tolerate it. You could not sleep at night. Everyone was up. The mosquito repellent must have done some good but not nearly enough. They just kept buzzing you and landing on you and biting you. The only thing that you could hear, besides the mosquitoes, was people slapping themselves. The sound could have been very dangerous except the Vietnamese weren't stupid enough to go into these areas.

Once when I was back in the rear I was rummaging in the supply tent. In one of the boxes there were mosquito hats. They were a soft hat with a circular brim and mosquito netting that came down to your shoulders and could be tied off. There were boxes of them. I figured typical army, they had them in the rear and forgot to send them to us. I grabbed what I could. When I got out to the field, I distributed them to my squad. The lieutenant asked where I got them. I told him that there were boxes of them in the rear.

We were in a mosquito infested area, what a pleasure they were. You could sleep, pull guard without being crazy. You did not have to constantly knock the mosquitoes off your face. The next day the lieutenant asked for enough for the whole platoon. To his surprise they refused to send them. They said that they were unsafe because of the mosquito netting that partially blocked your sight, therefore, were not warranted for use in combat. It seemed ridiculous. If you wore one it was like looking through a screen door at night. There might be some blockage but your vision was fine. If you weighed the pros and cons: the fact that you could not sleep would greatly diminish your effectiveness, the noise that was made not only from the slapping but the restlessness, it was no contest, but the army was adamant. They not only would not send out more, they wanted what we had back. They never persisted so we never turned them in. Eventually we moved out of that area. The mosquitoes were not the big problem. Most of the guys stopped carrying the hats, I kept mine. The whole thing was hard to believe.

The ants could also turn out to be a little bit of a pain in the neck. They had both black and red ants. The only time I encountered the black ants was that time I was shot at and dove into a nest. Ants completely covered my arm from my elbow to my fist but considering the circumstances they were only a minor annoyance. Red ants were a different story, they would bite you. Someone said that they really did not bite you, they just dig their back legs into your skin. It felt like a bite. The red ants did not just stay on the ground. On some trees they used to gather by the hundreds on the leaves. It must have been a food source to them.

One day on patrol I must have knocked into one of these leaves. The red ants fell onto the back of my neck, they all started biting. I felt the pain and started swatting them, dropped my rucksack and took off my shirt. The guy behind me started swatting them off. I was startled. This happened quite a few times to different guys in my unit.

Snakes were probably the most feared creatures over there. You were told about snakes that were so poisonous, their venom could kill you in thirty seconds. While I saw quite a few snakes most of them did not bother you. One day while walking on a rice paddy dike, someone must have stepped on a snake. It reared its head and started down the dike. Everyone jumped off the dike except this one guy. He kept running down the dike with the snake chasing him, finally he jumped. Everyone was laughing because it looked very funny. I am sure he did not think so. That is the only time I saw a snake bother anyone and I never knew of anyone being bitten by a snake.

They also had water buffaloes. Water buffaloes are basically peaceful animals that were used as work animals, resembling oxen. They were used to pull the carriages or plow the fields. Most of the time they just wallowed in the mud and water. Every once in a while they started charging, they were very frightening. It seemed that you would shoot them and they would just keep coming but eventually they would fall. The military had to pay the Vietnamese nine hundred dollars for each one that we killed.

Some areas were inundated with flies. They were usually near the villages. The sanitary conditions provided ample breeding habitat for the flies. In some villages they were so plentiful that they became really annoying, you were just constantly swatting them away. The Vietnamese did not seem to be bothered by them. The flies would land on them but they usually did not swat at them. They would just take it in stride. The flies would land but unless they were around the eyes or the mouth they just seemed to let them be. I guess you can get used to a lot of things.

Everything considered the environment caused a lot of problems for the American soldier. You were either hot or wet and then depending on where you were you had to contend with mosquitoes, leeches, snakes, flies, rats, and the occasional erratic water buffalo. All this led to a miserable existence. Then you had to deal with the enemy.

Coming from a modern industrial nation into a seemingly backward agricultural society could tend to lead towards an arrogance that would have you underestimate your enemy. In the early stages of the war this might have happened but if it did it was a grave mistake. The Vietnamese were a formidable enemy. They were crafty, cunning, hard working, diligent and persevering.

One day when we were out on patrol we came across an abandoned Viet Cong defensive position. It appeared to be set up for a squad sized operation. It looked like it had not been used for a while. The perimeter was roughly thirty or forty foot square and surrounding the perimeter were a multitude of pungi pits. Pungi pits were a primitive form of booby traps. They were basically a hole in the ground about two feet square and three feet deep. In the hole were placed a dozen or so bamboo shoots that were sticking up out of the ground and sharpened at the end like a spear. Although these weren't, if they had been functional they would have been covered so when someone stepped on the covering they would fall into the pit and be impaled by the bamboo shoots. The tips of the bamboo would be covered with human or animal feces so that not only would you be wounded by the bamboo shoots going through your body the feces, in theory, would release a poison into your body that could kill you.

Inside the perimeter there were about a dozen fox holes but their fox holes were different. Normally you would picture a fox hole about two foot wide, six foot long, and three to four feet deep. Now picture what theirs were like. They were about two foot wide, five foot long, and five to six feet deep. Then they would go in about three feet, up two to three feet, and back about one foot. If you could imagine the whole thing when they went back about one foot it created a ledge that could be used like a bed. They were extremely secured positions. They would probably stand a direct hit from a mortar. They probably would even be safe during a bombing raid. They would not survive a direct hit from a B52 but they would stand up to a lot of things. Even if you threw a grenade in, unless it landed just right, they would probably survive.

They were also set up in a way that you could walk right by them and not even know they were there. The blending in with the surrounding enhanced the effectiveness of the pungi pits.

I refer to the pungi pits as a primitive booby trap because by the time I got to Vietnam they were almost obsolete. Once the Vietnamese learned to use explosives they became masters at booby trapping. It seemed that there was nothing that they could not or would not booby trap.

Their booby traps ranged from simple devices, such as burying a bullet into the ground with a nail like device underneath and only the tip of the bullet above the ground. If you stepped on it, the bullet would hit the nail like device, acting as a firing pin, projecting the bullet through your foot.

They had a variety of booby traps that were set off by trip wires that crossed the paths that you would walk. It became policy that you would never touch anything that seemed discarded near a battlefield. If there was a weapon, or helmet, or even a body, {which was rare because they took their dead with them as much as possible) you would not touch it because the odds were that it was booby trapped. We use to carry grappling hooks that we would use to snare and move any foreign object before we would touch it.

They also used traditional devices such as anti-personnel mines. All in all they took the act of making booby traps and elevated it into an art form. Not knowing the statistics I would venture to say that more soldiers were wounded by booby traps than anything else. At least in the south.

They were very proficient at this but not always perfect. One day in returning across a path that we had crossed the night before we noticed a grenade with the pin out attached to the end of a trip wire. The grenade had not gone off because the handle was wedged against a small stump and there was not any room for it to disengage. Whoever set it was sloppy but we were very happy for his mistake.

The Vietnamese were very diligent and persevering. One day we captured a prisoner about twenty miles west of Saigon. He had a rocket strapped to his back, we turned him over to the Vietnamese. The next day the word came back that the prisoner had come from the Da Nang area. Da Nang is all the way up north not far from the D.M.Z. It seemed that this prisoner had traveled half the length of Vietnam with a rocket strapped to his back. His sole objective was to reach Saigon then fire his rocket into the city. It seemed like a long way to go just to fire one rocket but that is the way the Vietnamese were. They would go to extraordinary lengths to inflict injury upon the enemy.

There were many prisoners taken in Vietnam. Some would go through a Chu Houi program. This program was set up so that they could indoctrinate and brainwash the prisoners. After a couple of months they would send these prisoners out to work with the American armies.

The first time they sent a Chu Houi out to us we were all very skeptical. It was hard for us to believe that a Viet Cong or an N.V.A. regular was now on our side. How could you fight for one army one day and then against a couple of months later but they did. The first convert that they sent us spoke very little English. He was assigned to my squad. After about two weeks with us we were set up in N.D.P. outside of this village, when we took on machine gun fire. Everyone stayed low and returned fire except the convert. He stood up and returned fire. Then he grabbed the starlight scope, looked through it, spotted the enemy and returned fire. I was about five feet from the guy and had an M79. He wanted my weapon. Naturally I would not give it to him, so he stood up with the starlight scope and started directing my rounds. The enemy got away. No one was hurt. I looked at this guy and thought he was crazy. He showed no fear. After a while I got to know him pretty well. One day I saw him with his shirt off. He was riddled with bullet holes. I asked him how it happened. In broken English he explained how he was trying to shoot down a helicopter when he was hit by machine gun fire. That is how he was captured. He had about seven or eight holes in him. I do not know how he survived but he did.

The Chu Houis turned out to be an asset, they really hate the V.C. I do not know what brainwashing techniques they used against them but whatever it was they really worked. They helped in a lot of ways but their greatest asset was that they turned out to be tunnel rats.

The Vietnamese were masters of digging holes that turned into underground tunnels. Some of the tunnel complexes were extremely sophisticated. A tunnel rat was simply the guy who crawled into these tunnels to check for the enemy. A job nobody wanted to do but the Chu Houis seemed to relish it.

One day while on patrol we came across this small opening. It looked like it could be an opening to a tunnel. The Chu Houi crawled in taking with him only a 45. A couple of seconds later there were shots fired from inside the tunnel. We were about to enter when our Chu Houi came crawling out yelling, "V.C., V.C., I kill two V.C." He was very excited, he had a big smile on his face. He just kept saying, "I kill V.C." Like he wanted someone to pat him on the back. He went back into the tunnel with a squad behind him. My squad remained outside on guard. After ten minutes or so a few of the guys came out. They were saying you can't believe what is in there. There is a hospital in there. You have to see it. I asked the sergeant if I could go in. He told me to go ahead. I crawled into the opening. It was only about two feet in diameter and went back eight to ten feet. Then it opened into this big room just dug out of the dirt. Actually, there were three rooms as big as a large three room apartment. They were filled with bandages and medical supplies and of course the two dead V.C. I looked around in amazement thinking, how could they have built something like this underground? There were no support beams or anything. Just big rooms dug out of the earth. I went to the end of one of the rooms where I saw some natural light. I crawled into this small opening and looked up. It was the side of a well. Above me was light coming from the ground and below me was water. I crawled back into the hospital and then went back outside and walked around to where the well was. It looked like an ordinary well. I saw hundreds just like it. I looked inside and if I did not know what I was looking for I never would have spotted the hole in the side. It was amazing as I stood there looking around. There was a hospital below me yet you would never know it. The terrain looked as ordinary as any other in the area.

Although we came across others, this was the only complex I ever crawled into. Others were set up as military positions, tunnels that were set underground with small openings in strategic places. The enemy could fire upon you and you would never know where they were. The Vietnamese soldier was a truly remarkable adversary.

Since coming back to the States I have heard it said that American G.I.'s looked down upon the Vietnamese in a racist way probably because of the use of the word "Gook." I do not think this is a fair assessment, at least not for the combat veteran. While there I never heard of anyone speaking about the Vietnamese with anything but respect. We might have hated them because they were the enemy but we respected their abilities.

After the fall of Saigon I wondered what might have happened to the Chu Houis that were with us. I am sure that if they survived they were repatriated into the army. For being a soldier was what they knew, what they were, it is all that they ever did.

Although the Vietnamese could not beat us on the battlefield that were the true soldiers. We were merely biding our time.

This and That

What was unique to the infantry soldier in Vietnam that was different from past wars was the use of helicopters. The helicopters played an intricate role in the life of a combat soldier.

Helicopters were used for transportation, protection, emergency evacuations and supplies. The infantry soldier still traveled on his feet but helicopters were used to bring you from one area to another. This was done in what was called a combat assault. A combat assault was simply the helicopters landing you into an area and you disembarking in a combat ready formation. Most of the time it was just a matter of logistics and transportation and a very safe procedure. Once in a while they would land you in a hot L.Z. but good reconnaissance usually prevented that.

We made eighty some odd combat assaults while I was there. Not that I was counting but some people in the unit were. We were told that if you made over fifty combat assaults you would receive an air medal. As it turned out, you did receive an air medal if you made over fifty combat assaults but only if you were part of a helicopter crew.

One such combat assault turned into a very fiery situation. We were working up north and were on a combat assault into what we were told was a very bad area. Our instructions were that when we disembarked from the chopper we were to set up in formation and immediately start firing our weapons. This was called recon by fire. If any enemy were in the immediate area, they would either be hit, return fire, so we knew their location, or retreat. The chopper hovered a couple of feet off the ground. We disembarked and started firing. They had landed us in what was called elephant grass. This was tall, thick grass that was six, eight, ten foot or higher. The first wave of choppers pulled out and the second was coming in. We continued to fire our weapons. All of a sudden there was a fire. The area was very dry and one of the tracer bullets ignited the grass. The flames started spreading rapidly. The second wave of choppers pulled out without anyone disembarking. The flames were coming closer, the smoke was thick, we started to retreat. Behind us was another fire that must have been ignited by a different tracer round. Now there was fire all around us and it was spreading rapidly. There was nowhere to go. We moved in the direction of the second fire, hoping to find a stream or a hole or something. There was nothing. The first fire was pushing us towards the second fire which by now was a burning inferno. There was fire everywhere. We were trapped. Nobody started to panic but there was a feeling of helplessness. We were not sure what to do. It was only a matter of a minute or less before we would be completely engulfed by the flames. We decided that we were going to run as fast as we could in the direction of the least amount of fire and take our chances. We wet our clothes with water from the canteens. Then a chopper came. It positioned itself in a way that the wind from its blades was stopping the fire from advancing. Another chopper came and did the same thing. The rest came to rescue us. If it were not for the quick thinking of that chopper pilot we all would have been burned alive. As it was with the exception of a few people with some singed hairs, no one was hurt. We never got to meet that first pilot. If this gets published and you happen to read it, thank you.

About a month later one of the guys got a clipping from his hometown newspaper mailed to him. It said that first platoon of alpha company, 1/508 82nd Airborne was involved in a combat assault on such and such a date, killing, I forget how many, Vietcong. I wonder what they would have written if we had all burned to death.

Helicopters were life savers in many aspects. One of their greatest functions was that of evacuating the wounded from the battlefield. There were special choppers set up for this purpose but at times any chopper would do. They usually got there right away and evacuated the wounded swiftly. Countless lives were saved because of their proficiency.

There were, however, areas where they were not functional, that was up north in the mountains. Some areas were so thick with trees that they created double or triple canopies, it made it impossible for the choppers to land. It was so thick that you could not even blow down trees to create an L.Z.

One day Charlie Company hit contact and had wounded. There was no way to medivac them out. Our platoon was assigned to carry them down the mountain and find a place clear enough so that the engineers could blow an L.Z. We created make shift stretchers out of ponchos and tree branches. We all took turns carrying them. We walked for the better part of the day before we finally found a place clear enough to blow an L.Z. One chopper came in and took some of the wounded. It was a tight squeeze but he got in and out without much of a problem. A second chopper came and the rest of the wounded were put on board, he took off. It looked like he made it when one of the blades hit the top of a tree. The chopper crashed and everyone was killed. An empty feeling came over me. These were not the first dead American soldiers that I saw but they were the first to be killed right in front of my eyes. I watched the chopper fall but it seemed like slow motion. It did not seem that the crash could kill them but they were all dead. At first I had the feeling that this was not real. That something could be done to change it, then the reality set in. This realization of the finality of death, the fact it could occur at any time, under any circumstances, created an attitude in me that would try to consciously block the negative effects of death and continue with what had to be done. I did not try to pretend that it did not happen; I just realized that it was beyond my control, so I tried not to let it bother me. This attitude helped me in my control, and helped me in my initial confrontation with an immediate death. Although, when I had time for reflection, it usually affected me with a deep sense of loss and sometimes with a feeling of despair. At times it was difficult if not impossible to control the immediate feelings of hate and the want of revenge.

Another time we were working in this type of an area when one of the guys broke his ankle. He had to hump the bush for two days, using a make shift crutch, before he could be medivaced out.

One of the most pleasant sights that an infantryman could ever see was that of a helicopter gun ship. Again, working up north, sometimes they were not functional but down south they were life savers. They changed the nature of war. If you hit contact and you survived a couple of minutes until the gun ships arrived you were usually safe. They had remarkable fire power. They were equipped with rockets, grenade launchers, M60 machine guns, M50 machine guns. They would devastate an area. Ground troops would not stand a chance. That is why the enemy usually hit and ran. The gun ship was an infantryman's best friend especially because we had them and they didn't.

One day I was in a chopper when the pilot spotted three V.C. moving on the ground. He took the chopper down and the door gunner, equipped with an M60 machine gun, started firing. I was by the open door so I started firing my M79 at them. The pilot started yelling at me to stop firing. He said it was unsafe. I could not figure out why, but I stopped shooting. It did not matter, they did not need me, the door gunner got them.

As good as helicopters were there were times when they had a down side to them. On one combat assault they dropped us on a side of a mountain. They were hovering above some small trees about fifteen to twenty feet from the ground. The guy on the end was standing on the landing apparatus, pointing for the pilot to go down. The pilot kept shaking his head no and telling him to jump. The guy just kept pointing down, finally the gunner pushed him. I was next. When I saw how far it was I wanted to smack the gunner but I jumped. One guy jumped and the weight of the ruck sack came over his head and he wound up going head over heels down the mountain. Luckily he did not get hurt. This pilot could have come down another four or five feet without endangering his chopper, but he would not do it. Nice guy.

There were times that the pilots would not go into a hot L.Z. to get you out of there. I was only in country a couple of weeks when our company was pulling out of an area. My platoon was last. Everyone else was out then we started to be hit by mortars. The choppers refused to go back to get us. Our lieutenant was yelling and screaming over the radio. The mortars kept coming but they weren't accurate. Finally the choppers came and got us out.

There were other times when I saw choppers go into a hot L.Z., not the gun ships, the transport choppers. Then there were times when they would refuse to go in. I do not know if there was a standing policy against going into hot L.Z.'s or if it was up to the individual pilot but if you were waiting to get picked up or waiting for reinforcements and the pilots would not land, it would tend to piss you off. I heard guys talking about shooting at the choppers when in such situations.

When I got home to the states I used to break chops with a friend of mine, George Brown. He was in Nam roughly the same time I was. We used to correspond. On his second tour, he was a helicopter door gunner. I used to break his chops about how easy he had it, flying all day, sleeping in barracks at night, hot meals, women to clean your barracks and wash your clothes, cocktails every night, you guys had the life of Riley. I used to tell him that he was probably one of the guys who would steal our beer and soda, sell it to the Vietnamese, so they could sell it back to us. Friendly banter, but I used to break his chops. One day when I first got out of the service, George was working for this construction outfit, he asked me if I wanted to work a day. I went with him. My job was mixing cement by hand, George showed me how. After the first mix I was getting a little tired. By the third mix I thought my arms would fall off. George kept coming over and breaking my chops. "What's the matter 82nd Airborne, a little tired, afraid of a little work. I thought you guys were tough." I made a couple of more mixes, my arms were cramping, every muscle in my body was hurting. George kept breaking them, "You think us helicopter guys can't hack it? 82nd Airborne, let me show you how it's done!"

He mixed the batch of cement really fast. "What's the matter, you infantry guys can't keep up?" The rest of the day I continued mixing but I did not know where I got the strength from. I was in top shape but this work was hard. Finally the day ended. I had made fourteen mixes. We sat around having a couple of beers when one of the mechanics thanked George for bringing him such a good worker. "Hey George, remember your first day, you couldn't even finish the first mix." They laughed. I cursed at George, but he got me. George survived two tours in Nam but a couple of years later he was killed in a car crash. What George and I went through was merely a little friendly competition between veterans. To an outsider it might have looked like we were belittling each other's outfits but this was all in fun. War was not fun. There had to be an interdependency on each other for survival. If you perceived your survival as being threatened by the inaction of another party it is understandable how the focus of your frustrations can turn towards that party. Were the guys serious about shooting at their own choppers? I do not think so but survival can do strange things to you.

Helicopters were not the only means of transportation that we used in Nam. For a three to four week period while working in the delta region, we used to travel on a troop transport. They were like the landing barges that you used to see the marines come out of during invasions in the World War II movies. The type where the front lowers and everyone comes charging out. They are a lot bigger than they look in the movies. We used to travel on these things up and down the rivers in the Makong delta area. It was pretty good duty. We'd ride the river, the scenery was nice, like riding on a Circle Line cruise without the amenities. It stopped and you would still have to go on patrol, at night you still set ambushes but riding the rivers was very peaceful. We never got shot at. The only shooting that was ever done was by our captain. There were these beautiful white birds that used to fly by the rivers. He used to indiscriminately use them for target practice. It used to piss us off. I am not sure whether it was because he was the only one allowed to shoot at them or because we felt that there was no reason to kill these birds. I would like to think that it was the latter.

Loss of life due to accidents was an inevitable part of war. The artillery round that landed in the middle of our N.D.P, the Air Force bombing of the 101st were the worst but not the only accidents that occurred.

Actually, the 82nd was very accident conscious. They would take utmost precautions, like the handling of hand grenades, there were two prongs at the end on the pin that they would have you bend back. That was to stop the pin from easily coming out. You also had to secure the ring at the end of the pin so it was not dangling. That was so when you were on patrol a tree branch wouldn't inadvertently get caught and pull the pin out thereby blowing us up. Except for the worst areas, with the point man and machine gunner being an exception, they would not allow you to have a round in the chamber of your M16 and you were supposed to walk with your safety in the on position. You might think that it would be dangerous if you encountered the enemy but by the time you hit the ground you were locked and loaded and ready to fire. The M79ers were allowed to walk with a grenade in the chamber but you had to have it opened at the breach. When you were setting your claymore mines you always made sure that the end of the wire was capped. If left open a radio transmission could possibly detonate the mine. A claymore was an anti-personnel mine that would fire hundreds of pellets and had a back blast that if you were standing behind it would kill you. One day a guy was setting a claymore and he must have forgotten to cap it, the mine went off. He was standing a few feet away but luckily right to the side. The concussion jarred him and his ears were ringing for a while but otherwise he was very lucky he was not killed. I do not think anyone forgot to cap a mine after that. These precautions probably saved us from innumerable accidents.

Even with all the precautions that were stressed sometimes people got lackadaisical. One day our machine gunner handed his M60 to his ammo bearer to clean. He forgot to take the bullets out of the chamber. The ammo bearer also forgot to check to see if the chamber was cleared. He proceeded to clean the weapon and it went off and killed him. It was a tough thing for us to handle. Especially the machine gunner.

We were on patrol one time and all hell broke loose. Bullets were flying everywhere. About a minute later the word came down to cease firing. It seems that we were in a fire fight with our own reconnaissance platoon. We must have started it because recon was not supposed to initiate contact. I do not know if we were in the wrong area or they were or if it was a problem from the rear but somebody screwed up. Luckily, when we both called for choppers somebody in the rear was sharp enough to realize that we might be shooting at each other. No one was killed but a few people in recon were hurt.

I was only in country a couple of weeks at the time, we had just come back to fire base, it was daytime. There was nothing for us to do. I was tired so I went inside the bunker to catch up on some sleep. I was awakened by a loud noise. I felt a burning on the back of my leg and thought we were under attack. I heard something on the top of the bunker. I grabbed my weapon and slowly crawled out of the bunker, turned to fire, it was one of my own men up there. I almost blew him away. As it turned out he thought he was going to have some fun and scare the cherry. He unscrewed the blasting cap from the grenade, threw it down in front of the bunker, it bounced and exploded on my leg. He was scared because he thought I was going to shoot him. He was lucky I didn't in more ways than one. I had to go to the medic and have pieces of metal taken out of my leg. The officers read the whole platoon the riot act. That was the last accident caused by horseplay that I ever saw over there.

Just how many people were killed or wounded by accidents, we will never know but they accounted for many, many casualties.

This tidbit is for future soldiers who hopefully will never have to go to war but if you do and you want to get out of the field, snore.

We had a sergeant that came out to the field that was the loudest snorer I have ever heard. The first night that he was out we were on ambush and he started snoring. Very dangerous. We woke him up. He tried going back to sleep, he would snore, we would wake him up. Finally we just would not let him go to sleep. He was pissed but we were not going to let him get us killed. This went on for about a week. He caught a little sleep during the day but even then unless we were in a village he was so loud, you couldn't let him sleep. He became a real mess. You started to feel sorry for him, but what could you do? They finally removed him from the field. They did not tell us why but it did not take a genius to figure it out. A couple of guys were wondering if he was doing it on purpose but I really don't think so. If he was it was a great gimmick to get out of the field.

The one thing that everyone looked forward to was mail call. They would fly the mail out to the field as often as possible. Receiving a letter from home was reassuring and generally an uplifting experience. For most soldiers it was the best thing that could happen to them short of going home. Every time there was mail call you hoped that there would be a letter for you because not receiving any mail could become very demoralizing. For some, especially the married men, not receiving a letter could have an extremely negative effect on their attitude, but that would quickly change if they received a letter at the next mail call. If someone received a Dear John letter, or bad news from home, it could play havoc on their minds. The feelings of rejection or helplessness became compounded because of the confines of the environment that restricted your actions.

The military was fairly efficient in their handling of the mail but there were times when the mail was misdirected and might not catch up to you for weeks. That would have a negative impact on everyone. Mail call was a very important part in the life of a soldier.

I really do not mean to dwell on this but I have to get back to the physical demands that are placed upon an infantry soldier. You were walking all the time whether it was up and down mountains, through the jungle, or in rice paddies, in the heat or the rain or through mud and water. Then you were carrying a ruck sack on your back, in your ruck sack you had your food, water, ammunition, poncho, claymore, whatever other equipment that might have been needed plus any personal effects that you might want. The average ruck sack would weigh anywhere from forty to seventy pounds, depending on the ammo you were carrying. This weight was when it was dry no less wet. I would carry eight to ten quarts of water depending on where we were. This was on your back at all times when you were in the field.

Then there was a matter of sleep. When you were on ambush, which was most of the time, you set up in three or four man positions. In three man positions, you pulled guard one hour and slept two hours, pulled guard one hour, slept two hours. In a four man position sometimes you got two sets of three hours. Then you would get up and do it all over again, the next and the next day. That's not taking into account when you had contact. That night you might be on fifty percent or one hundred percent alert or just too damned scared to sleep.

When I was drafted I was six foot, one hundred and ninety five pounds. Sixteen weeks later after A.I.T. I was one hundred and eighty two pounds. When I went on R&R in Australia I got on a scale. One hundred and forty seven pounds with my clothes on. I thought the scale was broken. I found another. Same weight and that was with a couple of days of eating and drinking in me. I had not been that light since elementary school. The whole thing was just a very physically demanding experience.

There was one incident that really pissed everyone off. The rear jocks in their eternal wisdom issued a directive that every infantry soldier had to carry a body bag. A body bag was something that you were put in when you were killed. They wanted us to carry our own death bag. If you think about it, you would know how demoralizing that was, no less the extra weight. We all refused to carry them. They sent them out anyway. We left them at the L.Z. The officers did not say a word nor did they carry them. I never figured out why they would issue such a directive unless the sight of dead, perhaps mangled bodies were just too much for these rear area jocks to handle. We were bothered by that for quite a while.

We were working in the delta region, that was an area that was filled with streams, rivers and swamps. It was a fairly bad area and my squad was on point. The rivers were affected by the tides. When the tides came in the rivers rose. When the tides went out the rivers went down. We had to cross a small river, the river was down. It was an open area so we all charged across the river. When we got to the other bank we all sank in the mud. We could not get out. We were standing there like sitting ducks in mud up to our hips. The more you tried to pull out the more you seemed to sink. It took about five minutes but finally, using all the strength I could muster, pulled out one leg. I sort of knelt on the mud sideways trying to free my other leg. The leg I was kneeling on started sinking. I pulled out my other leg and then crawled across the mud. It was only a couple of feet to dry ground. I got there, extended my weapon and pulled another guy out. By this time someone else had freed himself. I went to pull security. We had to meet the rest of the platoon a little further down the river where they could cross. They were laughing and breaking our chops. It probably was a funny sight to see seven or eight soldiers stuck in the mud. I did not think so at the time.

The first day that we had ever worked in this area they issued us air mattresses. That night we pulled ambush on the edge of a river. We all blew up our air mattresses and slept on them. It felt good not sleeping on the ground. We were all awakened by the guy on guard. The tide had come in and one of the guys, still asleep, was floating down the river. We could not yell at him, one of the guys threw a rock, it missed but he woke up anyway. He was at least forty yards down the river, probably very disoriented when he woke up but he made it back to the shore. I don't know what would have happened if he kept sleeping. We stopped using air mattresses after that, not because of this incident, but they just made too much noise when using them.

If you did not believe in evolution before we worked in the delta region there was a strong argument for it there. In some areas when the tides went out, they would completely empty the river. There would be nothing but mud and some residual pockets of water.

We were sitting on the bank of an empty river when I saw this fish, it was sitting in the mud. Then it started to walk. It would use its fins as legs to move around. Then I saw a couple more of them all doing the same thing. They could have gone out with the tide like the rest of the fish but through some evolutionary process they learned how to survive in the mud. I do not know how they were breathing, I guess their gills could extract enough oxygen from the mud. It was the strangest sight to see fish walking.

Social evolution also started to hit some parts of Vietnam. The villages closest to Saigon were starting to get electricity. They would have one television per village. Their means of transportation went from walking and oxcarts to mopeds and motorcycles, at least near Saigon. Their booby traps went from sticks and pungi pits to high explosives. They were becoming part of the twentieth century. I could not help wonder if they were better off the way they were. Except for the war they seemed to be a peaceful, happy, family oriented people that adapted well to their environment. They produced enough food to feed their families and seemed to enjoy their village lifestyle. Now they were being inundated with the progress of the twentieth century. I couldn't help wonder if this progress was going to be beneficial or if they would be better off as an anachronism. I am still not sure but I guess you cannot stop social evolution even if it might not be progress.

Combat

One of the most often asked questions of any veteran is, "Did you see combat?" The person asking the question usually has a preconceived notion of what they think combat is all about and tries to extract responses that will either reinforce that notion or illuminate their quest to understanding the combat experience. Usually the question is very judgmental in that if they get a negative response they will categorize the person as not really being part of a war. That categorization is unjust. They usually follow with questions like: Were you wounded? Did you kill anyone? What's it like to be in combat? Most combat veterans will usually refrain from entertaining such discussions but not usually for the reasons that people think, that the combat veteran does not want to talk about it because it will bring back painful memories. Those memories are there and painful or not they are not going to go away because you don't talk about them. They are part of your life experience but to be able to articulate that experience to a non-combatant and to communicate it in a way that there will be a mutual understanding is difficult if not impossible.

I will attempt to bring you to a better understanding by dealing with combat in general and then try to take you through one of my worst experiences.

First of all, whether you were wounded or if you killed someone, that's only one aspect of the combat experience. The question, what is it like to be in combat, has to restructured to ask, what was it like for you in a particular combat situation? The word combat is a general term. Each combat experience is different and peculiar to the individual that was involved. You could be in the same company, same platoon, same squad, same fire fight, and have a different experience than others that were with you.

If you look at the wars of the twentieth century, by their nature, the experience has to be different. In WWI you basically dealt in trench warfare and artillery attacks. WWII was the most diverse, dealing anywhere from large-scale battles to hand to hand combat, jungle type warfare, tank, air, and naval battles. The Korean War, whose combat veterans per capita probably saw more action than any other veteran, had to deal with massive waves of people. The Vietnam veteran depending on time and place dealt with jungle warfare, terrorism, and large scale battles.

Although each experience is unique and different there are certain aspects that are common to most combat veterans. Fear and your reaction to it was probably the same in all wars. By that I mean that fear and your reaction to it is an individual thing. Yet every combat veteran, regardless of the war had to experience it.

You're put into a situation where you have to confront death. Either the possibility of you dying, one of your buddies or the enemy you might kill, that's common to all combat veterans. The working as a unit to ensure each individual's survival and as an individual to ensure the survival of the unit. The fact that you can transcend your individuality for the survival of your unit is common to most combat veterans in every war. Being under attack or attacking, killing or being a part of a killing force, seeing men wounded or die, experience emotions that are elevated to a level that can only be attained in combat, all of these things create a common experience and bond among combat veterans.

Combat in Vietnam had its own uniqueness. During my first four months we were working the I Corp area, basically mopping up the aftermath of the Tet offensive. The Tet offensive was an all out affront by the North Vietnamese army and the Viet Cong. It was their greatest offensive maneuver of the war and they were soundly defeated. The marines in the I Corp area did an outstanding job in repelling the N.V.A. and driving them back towards North Vietnam.

I worked the area roughly from June through October 1968. By that time the N.V.A. was basically on the run. We would work search and destroy missions constantly pursuing the enemy. We met up with light resistance that was meant to detain us so that the major body of the N.V.A. could retreat into neutral areas.

Although they were still engaging in sapper attacks, mortar attacks, occasional ambushes, and fire-fights, their offensive capabilities were basically decimated. By the time we left the area, with perhaps the exception of small pockets of resistance, the N.V.A. had withdrawn from the I Corp area. Unfortunately we were not allowed to pursue, thereby giving them time to regroup and to come back to fight another day.

Down south was a whole different ball game. The resistance went from little to none outside of Saigon to very heavy in the Macong delta area. The war however was different. It was not one army engaging or pursuing the other army. It was us pursuing the Viet Cong, with them usually picking the time and place that they would choose to engage us in their hit and run type tactics. The Viet Cong were not a standing army. They were more like loose knit bands of guerillas that would look to inflict their punishment and then retreat. It wasn't one army fighting another army in a prolonged battle.

Our basic operations were us seeking out the V.C. in search and destroy missions and setting ambushes at night. We would occasionally catch them off guard but they were the ones that usually initiated contact. They had three basic offensive modes. They would hit you with mortar or rocket attacks that usually took place at night. They would booby trap an area, anything from villages to trails to any discarded object. Their third mode was to set up an ambush hitting you with as much as they had as quickly as they could usually booby trapping their escape route. The secret to surviving these types of ambushes was to hit the ground as quickly as possible almost on instinct. When you heard the sound of a bullet you would be on the ground before your brain actually comprehended what the sound was. Then you would immediately return fire. Technically each person had their job to do and if it was done properly, you would command fire power superiority very quickly. Then in pursuing the enemy you had to be extremely careful of booby traps. They were very proficient in the types and the placement of the traps that they set.

Most encounters usually only lasted a matter of minutes. That was due not only to our ground troops' superior fire power but to the helicopter gun ships and at times the Air Force. They would come in with such fire power that the V.C. would look to retreat before they got there, which on good days, was only a matter of minutes. So if you survived the initial contact and reacted in the proper manner you came out of it all right.

The next part of our strategy might seem appalling but it became an intricate part of our survival. It led to burning of villages, grabbing a kid and putting a gun to their head and having him walk you through a booby trapped area, calling on artillery and air support to decimate an area that might or might not be occupied by so called civilians. I know that this is hard to comprehend as being justified but let me try to put it into some type of perspective.

Let's take the bully on the block. When you were a kid the old adage was that if a bully was picking on you, to fight back and even if you lost, the bully would stop picking on you and find someone else to bully. Good strategy but what happens if the bully is not a coward, but a legitimate tough guy who comes back to fight you the next day and the next. You cannot go around getting beat up every day, what are your options? You could go to the police but let's say they're not a factor. You could run and hide but what happens if you eventually run into him? You could become his patsy but that's no way to live or you could get a baseball bat and beat him until he cries uncle then hit him again so he knows you mean it. This alternative could escalate until one of you is dead or the bully could gain fear or respect for you where he would leave you alone. In our so called civilized society there should be ways of dealing with a situation before it escalates to that level but what do you do in war?

Let's say the V.C. is the bully, it's already a given that it has escalated to the point where you are going to kill each other. Even though you have the superior force, they have the upper hand, they're not engaging you in a battle with all their forces against all your forces and see who wins. They're picking their spots, inflicting as much punishment as possible then running away in order to counteract that you had to gain fear and respect from him. If they set a booby trap in a village, you burn down his village. I mean his village, because if it was friendly it would not be booby trapped or they would let you know about them. If you are working in an area that you see a booby trap or suspect of being booby trapped and you see a kid, you grab him, put a rifle to his head and have him walk you through the area. No one will get hurt. He knows where the booby traps are. The V.C. didn't want to blow up their own children. If he walks you into an ambush, which I never saw happen, good-bye kid. If they persist in ambushing you call in an air strike and blow away the surrounding area.

You knew that they were tough so you had to show them that you were not only tough but tougher than they were. Eventually either out of fear or respect they would leave you alone and bother another unit that might not act in this manner. If all the units acted this way and they allowed us to pursue across borders the war could have ended with us victorious, but that wasn't the case. Our objective in combat was survival, and this is what we had to do to survive. The nature of war itself creates ugly, nasty, seemingly morally unacceptable situations. The combat soldier is part of this nature of war. His right to survival supersedes many of these seemingly morally unacceptable situations.

There was a famous news reel about a soldier using his zippo lighter to burn down a village. The whole country from the president on down was aghast, I guess without being there you couldn't understand what was going on but in our recent conflict in Iraq we watched bombings where hundreds of thousands of people were killed. Tens of thousands of so called innocent civilians and we applauded. If we had to fight Iraq I am glad that it was fought that way but are we that fickle as a people or is effective P.R. the dictator of our conscience?

During the Vietnam war there was a liberal, anti-war slant to the press. They would portray acts of war from a civilian moralistic viewpoint, thereby superimposing a moralistic standard that appeared acceptable to the general population. In combat, these moralistic standards could be contrary to your survival. Survival must take precedence.

During the Persian Gulf War, there was a pro-war slant to the press. They assured us that every precaution was being taken to prevent the loss of civilian life. This became an acceptable moral standard for the general population. When it became known that tens of thousands of civilians were killed during our bombing raids people accepted this as being an unfortunate consequence of war. Especially since the overall missions insured the survival of our ground forces.

Two wars, two points of view. To the combat soldier there can only be one point of view, survival. How the press relations were handled to make the unfortunate consequences of war more or less palatable to the general population was not part of his domain.

One of the main factors in any combat situation is discipline. The training and discipline that you receive stateside is invaluable and that discipline must be maintained in combat situations.

This might seem a little contradictory from the way I have portrayed my individuality and dealings with authority throughout this book but you learn to separate field operations from the rest of the situations. Even in field operations there is leeway to question and voice opinions but in combat there is no leeway. Things happen so fast that you only have time to react. While you are in a reactionary mode you must be disciplined to do your job and obey the orders that you are given. Your life and the lives of people you are with depend on it. Usually you just react and know what to do but if an order is given, deviating from your reaction there can be no hesitation. It must be obeyed without question. Hopefully the person giving the orders knows what they are doing because you cannot take time out to decide that. In combat it is very easy for things to become chaotic. Bullets are flying, the noise is deafening, you might not realize where you are being hit from, people could be getting wounded or killed, discipline and adherence to orders must prevail in order to prevent a bad situation from becoming out of control. Plus every situation is different, you could be cut off from the leadership, or they could be hit and someone else has to take charge. You could be the point man and from your vantage point you might initially have to direct what's going on. Things happen so fast that you initially have to react as an individual and then collectively as a unit. Hopefully everyone has a discipline and the wherewithal to act in the proper manner because you could very easily lose your head. Literally and figuratively. No matter how much you prepare or how seasoned you are you still must deal with your emotions. Emotions aren't something that you can turn off or on like a water faucet. The nature of combat automatically sparks emotions that can be brought to unparalleled levels yet must be controlled. An adrenaline runs through you that just heightens your susceptibility to a variety of possible emotions that might emerge. Fear, hate, survival, rage, compassion, loneliness, insecurity, any one of these or all of them or emotions that I am not even articulating can be manifesting themselves in your consciousness which is already at such a heightened state that if they are not contained they will become paramount causing you to lose control. Simply put, one emotion or another would take control of your consciousness thereby causing you to act in an improper manner. A combat soldier either has to have no emotions, which is unlikely, or a high degree of mental discipline to control the emotions in order to function in the proper manner. This degree of mental discipline is necessary but not necessarily easy to attain.

Most non-combatants would assume that fear was the emotion that would be hardest to control but that really wasn't the situation. In your initial combat experience fear might have been the emotion that you initially had to control but with few exceptions most soldiers dealt with their fear. Other emotions could bring you to such a heightened state that you could experience a new dimension of these emotions that could take control before you became aware of your need to control those emotions.

The 82nd Airborne as a unit saw its share of combat, but there were other units that saw more. If your unit is involved in combat, you are part of that unit, but you might not necessarily be involved in actual combat. For example, while we were working up north we were usually involved in company sized operations. You could be in the point squad of the first platoon and hit contact but the people in the last squad of the fourth platoon could be so far removed that with the exception of the sound they would have no idea that a fire fight was taking place. Conversely the rear platoon could be hit by ambush and the point platoon would not be involved. The fighting usually didn't sustain itself long enough to where one would have time to help the other. Your company might hit contact three days in a row and depending on how lucky you were you could be involved in all of it or none of it. I don't want to be misleading; it's not that you would not be a participant, for you would probably be involved in sweeping the area or pursuing the enemy, but as far as actually being fired upon or seeing the enemy and returning fire, you might not be involved.

There have been soldiers that have seen a disproportionate amount of combat for the amount of action that their unit saw. Then others who saw little or none in spite of the fact that their units might have been heavily involved. I would look upon this as the luck of the draw, others would say for the grace of God.

This is going to be a very argumentative point but God had nothing to do with who survived in combat. There was no divine intervention on behalf of one soldier or another. The unit that was most disciplined and could command superiority in fire power would win the battle. I think it was Napoleon who stated that God is on the side of the army with the biggest legions. Don't take this as being atheistic because it is not meant that way. As I stated earlier they say that there are no atheists in fox holes. That's probably because any one with any kind of religious background, when they become scared, turn to God because that is the alternative that they know. In combat there is no time for fear, before and after, but usually not during. A good soldier automatically transcends that fear even though it's probably the most fearful situation you could be in. You do not put yourself in the hands of God but you rely on yourself and the people you are with for your survival. If someone gets wounded it is because the enemy had the advantage or you made a mistake, not because God willed it. I can perceive many arguments counter to this but if there really was divine intervention when you are shot at why duck? Why not just stand up and walk towards the enemy? If it's your time to go, he will kill you, if not you will him. It does not work that way.

Most combat veterans know instances where people were very lucky and could have been killed but weren't. They probably attribute that to God because why else did it happen that way? This could cause endless discussions but for myself I know there is no divine intervention in warfare. Jesus was once asked about paying tribute to Caesar, he replied, "Render unto Caesar the things that are Caesar's, and to God the things that are God's." War, in spite of its life and death nature, belongs to Caesar.

A lot of veterans probably did not look at it this way and at times I am sure there was a lot of praying going on but the more experienced you became deep down you realized the key to your survival was in your hands and those of the people around you.

We were working in the delta area, a different section than we had been working. I was in country almost eleven months at the time. We were working in a company sized operation. It was a bad area and everyone was a little on edge. I was walking point that day, not the greatest situation but better than walking second because if you hit a booby trap, you have no one to blame but yourself. Walking point was easy in some areas and difficult in others. This was an area that called for extreme caution. We were working our way around the village and into the bush, a thick shrub, low tree lined type of area. It seemed like I was walking extremely slow that day, aware of everything that was around me. My consciousness was in a heightened state. My primary concern was booby traps. Constantly looking down in order to spot the traps yet at the same time observing everything around me to make sure I didn't walk into an ambush. I had just approached the outskirts of a tree lined area when the lieutenant called for us to take a break. I did not like the area ahead and was looking to see if there was a way around it when the lieutenant called me back to his position. He had the map out and wanted to go over the route that we were going to take. I told him that there was thick brush dead ahead and would like to try to work our way around it. Then a barrage of shots rang out. I hit the ground and faced in the direction of the sound. More shots. I fired a grenade into the area then reloaded. About ten yards to my left and maybe fifteen yards ahead, I noticed my squad leader, an instant N.C.O., new to the field, got up and started to pursue from my left to right. The rest of the squad was following. At the same time I spotted two V.C. moving the same way. They were dead ahead about thirty to forty yards. I pumped a grenade at them then another. I saw no more movement but I am not sure whether or not I had hit them. By now bullets were flying heavily in both directions. Maybe twenty seconds had passed. Then there was a series of explosions. It came from the area that my squad was entering. Another sergeant was yelling for everyone to stay down. There was movement by our guys to my right. The sergeant ran across the booby trapped area, exploding one, to take control. More explosions. I fired a few more rounds. By now, the lieutenant was on the horn calling for air support, the sergeant had taken control of the front lines, people were yelling for medics, heavy firing, the only bullets I was hearing were coming from us, none coming in our direction. I went to fire another round when I saw this person coming towards me, it was the sergeant from the second squad, another instant N.C.O., new to the field, he was hit pretty bad. He was disoriented and kept coming towards me. He was bleeding heavily. I jumped up and grabbed him and knocked him to the ground. It wound up that I was lying on top of him. A barrage of automatic weapons came flying right over our heads, we were in the open. I managed to get off a couple of rounds but I really did not want to lift up my head. The sergeant was unconscious. The automatic weapon fire lasted a good twenty seconds then it stopped. I rolled off of the sergeant and continued to fire. By now we were laying down extremely heavy fire and they had stopped. Maybe two minutes or so passed. We continued firing, people were yelling for medics, I yelled for a medic, but there were not enough to go around. A helicopter just happened to be passing by and landed to see if he could help. Our fire was continuing. The lieutenant was yelling to put any badly wounded on the chopper. I heard him but I doubt the people up front did. I went to pick up the sergeant. He was unconscious but alive. Someone came over to give me a hand and we dragged him to the chopper. I got into the chopper and we got him in. As I released his arms, his head fell to the side. There was this gaping hole in his neck that had stopped bleeding. I was not sure if he was dead or alive so I reached down, he was breathing slightly. I wanted to stay with him but there was probably not much I could have done. The chopper was ready to take off . The guy with me was yelling for me to get off. I thought that there should be somebody there with him but what could I do? I jumped off.

I went towards my squad, by now I think the firing had stopped. The ChuHoi came up to me and handed me the squad leader's rifle. He shook his head saying no, meaning that he was dead. I asked by name about the rest of the squad. There were three or four that were wounded but he indicated that they were okay. Then one guy in the squad came up and started yelling at me, "Where were you? You were supposed to be on point. Everybody's hit. Where were you?"

"I was with the lieutenant."

At that point the sergeant who took control yelled for me to come forward. "Prep that area with grenades." It was the heavy bush area, the one I wanted to go around. I stated walking towards it firing grenades. I would fire, reload, fire, reload, the whole time walking towards the area. My mind was going a mile a minute. I was building into a highly emotional state. I was mad and frustrated and just wanted to kill. What the hell did he mean where was I? I just kept walking and firing. The whole battle went through my mind. My mind jumped from the sergeant that I left on the chopper, to my squad, to the V.C. There was a rage in me, a hate. Where were those bastards? I saw a trail of blood and started to follow, hoping to kill anything that was there. The sergeant was yelling for me to come back. I sort of heard him but I was not really cognizant of him. The rage and hate and the desire to kill were controlling my actions. I entered into a different reality. He must have called six or seven times before I snapped out of it. I ran back towards him. He looked at me and asked if I was all right. I shook my head yes but the emotions that I had just experienced were overwhelming.

By now, the gun ships were there and we were pulling back, then the Air Force came, two jet fighters. We regrouped and watched the attack. It was devastating. The bombs and the rockets and whatever else were just pounding the area. My mind still would not slow down. A million thoughts were running through it. What the hell just happened? We were just caught off guard. People were making moves that they just should not have been making. My squad leader is dead. Three quarters of my squad is wounded, others were badly hurt. My buddy is yelling at me, I lost control for the first time in my life. When I was walking towards the bush, prepping the area, I was in such an emotional state that I really did not realize what was going on. The hate and frustration caused by the combat situation created a rage in me, but the catalyst that put me into a different dimension was probably my buddy's questioning of me. The desire to kill the enemy was my only focus and that focus took control of my actions. I was in a different state of consciousness. I was not looking for booby traps, I was not focused on safety or survival; I just wanted to kill one of those bastards. There was not even a reason for me to be walking. I could have prepped the area from where I was. I was fortunate that the sergeant kept calling me and brought me back to a normal conscious state because who knows where my mind might have taken me.

Whose fault was all of this? If I had been on point, assuming that I would not have been killed on the initial contact, probably none of this would have happened the way it did. Not that I had been in that many fire fights but I was seasoned, my reactions were always good. They sent out a cherry, who had been to school for ninety days and put him in charge. He made an error in judgment. The first thing you do is get down and then maintain fire power superiority, not pursue. Even if it was time for pursuit, you knew that they were going to booby trap their escape route. Every other guy in the squad was seasoned and knew what to do but in combat you have to follow orders. He gave the wrong order.

If I was on point I would have taken control and nobody would have been pursuing. I knew survival was the name of the game, not being a hero. This shouldn't sound like I am taking any blame because that probably belonged to the army for having such a system that put an instant N.C.O. in charge of a combat unit. Even the new officers would usually defer to the sergeant until they got their feet wet or maybe the blame belongs to John Wayne for making all those movies that glorified war and made it look like a game. The sergeant looked liked someone in one of those movies. Gung-Ho, running across battlefields. Unfortunately, it cost him his life and caused others to be wounded. Some game.

Then there was the other instant N.C.O., the sergeant that I put on the chopper. Why he was where he was is a mystery, he should not have been there. The whole damn thing was a mess. I just kept running things through my mind while watching the Air Force do its thing. Then the guy who was yelling at me came over, "Listen, I did not mean anything by that." We looked at each other. I shrugged my shoulders. We both knew what just happened was a tough experience.

Then I started thinking, how lucky I was that the lieutenant called for a break at that exact time. I must have been only a few feet from the V.C. I did not see them but they were there. Another couple of seconds and they would have sprung the ambush on me. Was somebody up there looking out for me? It would be nice to think so but awfully arrogant to think that I would be spared so that someone else would die. No, I was just lucky.

The Air Force continued their barrage. If you saw the amount of explosives that were dropped on the area you would have to assume that nothing could live through the bombardment. After a half hour or so, the Air Force withdrew and lo and behold a bunch of women and children came walking out of the area towards us. The machine gunner initially started to fire but the captain immediately put a stop to it. How these people survived that bombardment is hard to explain. Their village was a little to the right and maybe the Air Force avoided them but I do not see how. They were probably all in shelters that were dug out under the huts but I never got to see. My platoon didn't sweep the area, another platoon did. They came back with some type of high body count. Whether it was real or not is anybody's guess.

I calmed down to relative normalcy. We continued on patrol and pulled ambush that night. Just another day I guess but it was one that we all wished had never happened. We never really talked that much about it. As far as the guys that were wounded, I never got to see them again. The sergeant that we put on the chopper, I believe he lived but I am not really sure. I do not remember going to a memorial service for him but I do not recall the service for my squad leader either. I was only out in the field another three or four weeks after that and during that time the V.C. did not mess with us. I do not know if it was because we were lucky or after the devastation that was put upon that area they decided to leave us alone.

Everybody's experience in combat is different and how it affects that person only that individual is capable of knowing, but the experience in one way or another will change your life forever.

The military must do what it has to in order to maintain an effective fighting machine but to glorify combat is one of the biggest misconceptions ever to be perpetrated on man.

Coming Home

The only sight that would always put a smile on your face was of that of a freedom bird. A freedom bird was a jet that was taking people back to the world. We did not see them often but when we did they offered a ray of hope. Everyone kept a short-timers calendar, counting the days till you went home. Some of them were very elaborate. I kept mine in my head.

Going home became more and more of a reality the shorter you became. It affected you in many ways. You became very aware and alert to what was going on. You became a little afraid. Not the fear that you experienced when you first got there or even like that of being in a combat situation. It was more like you became nervous. You wanted to make sure that everything was done right. You knew that you had made it to that point and you wanted to make sure you were going home.

It was now the middle of May and a lot of people that I was with were starting to go home. They started sending a bunch of cherries out to the field. They sent one guy out who probably shouldn't have been there. He was very immature. One night while we were on ambush we were in two positions. I was on guard on one and he was in the other. I looked over and saw him sleeping. I was going to low crawl over there but I figured he might wake up and shoot me. I picked up a small rock and threw it at him. He woke up. The next morning I gave him hell. I ranted and raved and screamed at him, explaining what I would do if I ever caught him sleeping again. I am not sure that he understood the seriousness of it.

We came back to a fire base. A couple of us went over to the artillery, had a couple of beers, and got high. I went back to check on the guard positions, not necessarily my job, but I was short and nervous. As I walked to the bunker, I saw a silhouette of the same guy. He looked like he was sleeping. I snuck up on him. If he was sleeping I was going to knock him off the bunker. I climbed up on the bunker and he was asleep. I cocked my fist and moved towards him when there was this big explosion right in front of us. I jumped off the bunker yelling, "Incoming!" By the time I hit the ground I started to put together what had happened. While sneaking up on this guy I stepped on the detonator for the claymore mine which in turn exploded the phoo gas in front of us. I went to the radio and called it in as an accident not incoming. Thet I went over to the cherry on guard. He was a nervous wreck, he didn't know what happened. I started to yell at him when they called me to C.Q. When I got to the command quarters they asked what had happened. I told them I was checking the guard position when I accidentally stepped on the detonator. They asked who was on guard. I told them but I did not tell them that he was asleep. They knew that I had yelled at this guy a couple of days prior and assumed that he was sleeping so I detonated the claymore to scare the hell out of him. I told them that it was an accident and left it at that. The guy stayed clear of me. I was not out in the field that much longer but to my knowledge he never fell asleep again. I do not know if he made it or not but I tend to doubt it. I hope he did. That was the last time I got high at a fire base.

I had put in for a seven day leave. That was an R&R but it was your second one. It was not automatic but field soldiers were rarely turned down. The word came that they had turned me down. I was pissed. I went to the lieutenant and asked him why I was turned down. He told me that I made too many waves. That I had ruffled too many feathers with the brass and they weren't going to grant me any privileges. I told him that was bullshit. I looked him in the eye and told him that I was a good soldier, that he knew that and I deserved this leave. He didn't say anything and then said come with me. He took me to the captain and pleaded my case. He told him that I was one of the best that he had and didn't know why they were treating me this way. He reminded him how I saved everybody's ass the day that we were all immersed in water in the rice paddy. He also gave me a few other compliments. The captain listened. He turned to me and said, "Coughlin, I do not want you getting lost in the rear. I am going to let you go, but you have three days to get there, seven days on leave and three days to get back. Then I want you back in the field. Is that clear?"

"Yes, sir."

"Take the next chopper out, but I want to see you back here on time."

"Yes, sir. Thank you sir."

On the way out on the chopper I couldn't have been happier. I was shocked at how the lieutenant stood up for me. It made me feel very good. The captain must have been reading my mind because I did not know how but I was not planning on going back out to the field.

I got to the rear and could have wasted a day in Saigon, but I was taking no chances. I was not going to give them the opportunity to cancel my leave. I got the hell out of there. I spent seven days in Hong Kong, a little expensive but a very enjoyable place. Nice women, good food, and I got the opportunity to call home. Then it was over, back to Vietnam. They landed us in Bien Hoa. I wasted a couple of days there but I had to go back to my unit.

The whole time I was trying to figure out how I could avoid returning to the field. I was a very short timer but I knew that they would not let me stay back in Ton Sun Nhut. The first day back I went on sick call, the first time that I ever did that other than for dental problems. Back when we were up north I hurt something in my buttocks. It was like I pulled muscle but different. It bothered me at times but I could live with it. They sent me to a field hospital in Saigon. I told the doctor that it happened when we were humping the mountains up north and now it was really bothering me. He examined me and then told me that he was going to send me to Japan for an operation. I asked him what it entailed. He explained it to me and said it was a tricky operation that could entail a lot of physical therapy during recovery. I told him that I really didn't want an operation, besides I was going home in eighteen days and didn't want anything to prevent that. I asked him if he could give me eighteen days of light duty. Not only did he give me a light duty slip, he wrote it into my medical records. Then he told me to have it looked at when I got stateside.

I could not believe it, no more field! My last eighteen days spent in Ton Son Nhut and Saigon. Not a bad way to spend the end of my tour. Even if they gave me some menial task to do and I could not get into Saigon, who cared? No more field!

I could hardly wait to see their reaction. I knew that they were going to blow up over this. I got back and showed it to the first sergeant, he went crazy. "The captain told me to have you back in the field as soon as you got here. I'll see about this." He checked with our doctor, then with the doctor in Saigon, but it was in my medical records. There was not much he could do about it. Light duty was light duty. That night I was going to go to Saigon but I figured I better not push my luck.

The next day Top told me to gear up, that he was sending me out to a fire base. I told him he couldn't do that. I was on light duty, but he was prepared. He had the doctor there and said it was permissible to send someone on light duty out to a fire base. I told them that I wanted to go back to the hospital in Saigon. They said that the fire base had adequate facilities. Now there was not much that I could do. I could refuse to go but a court martial was not an attractive option anymore. I figured, what the hell? A fire base was a fairly safe place anyway. I geared up and got on the chopper.

When we got to the fire base we were in a completely different area than I had ever been in before. It was a very bad area. It was not much of a fire base. They told me that it had been hit and that my unit had hit contact while I was away. This was where I was going to spend the end of my tour. I couldn't believe it. There was nothing for me to do except to pull guard and worry. I wondered if I would have been better off in the field with my unit but light duty prevented that. I was just there counting the days. I would watch people from my unit come back and go home. I was just there. There was a feeling of frustration and helplessness. Then came June 22. My original deros date and I am out in this God forsaken fire base with nothing to do but let it play on my mind. Another couple of days passed and then that night we got mortared. I do not know if I was more scared or more frustrated. I just kept thinking while we were under attack that I should be home but now is when something is going to happen. I was going to lose my life or my legs. How stupid could I be? Why didn't I just go to Japan? Finally they stopped. They really weren't that close but I just could not believe it. What the hell was going on? If I went to Japan, I could have refused the operation and they would have sent me home. Stupid! Stupid! Stupid!

Another couple of days passed and they finally sent a chopper to bring me to the rear. I should have been ecstatic but I was more in a daze. The last two weeks was like a mental torture. They started processing me out. They gave me my rifle, a Chinese S.K.S to take home. Then they said that orders were never cut for my army accommodation medal or my bronze star. They were processing them now and they would follow me to my next duty station which was supposed to be Fort Benning, Georgia. Then it was off to Bien Hoa. There were a couple of us leaving at the same time. I started to realize that I was actually gong home but I was still very leery. Finally I got on the freedom bird. We made a stop in Alaska then back to San Francisco. I got off the plane then went into the air base when I started to shake. I was shaking uncontrollably. A sergeant came up and tried to help but I couldn't stop shaking. I guess the whole war was just coming out of me. It lasted for at least ten minutes, then I finally calmed down.

They processed me out in a couple of hours, and then I called home. My family wanted to pick me up at the airport but I told them I had to fly stand by and did not know when I would arrive. I got on the first flight that I tried for a non-stop directly from San Francisco to Kennedy Airport. It was a pleasant flight. The stewardesses were friendly and I sort of took inventory on myself.

I was alive, all my body parts were intact, I was thinking clearly and feeling normal. I did it, I survived! Now I am on my way home! What a great feeling! I was higher than the plane.

We landed at Kennedy, then I got a cab. It was only about a half-hour to my home. I started talking to the cab driver, explaining that I had just come from Vietnam. He said, "Oh, that's why you have the rifle." I saw that he was little nervous. I should have bought a case for it but I guess I was so used to having a weapon in my hands that I did not think of it. Then we were driving down my block. It looked the same. We stopped in front of my house, I paid the driver, got out and looked around. There were signs and banners in some of the neighbors windows saying "Welcome Home Danny". Then I heard screams from my house. Danny's home! Danny's home! My whole family came out to greet me. Then some neighbors came rushing out. It was a very nice greeting. I went into the house and talked to my family. It felt great to be home.

That day and into the night I talked with my family and some friends. Later that night I went outside to get some air. I was going down my stoop when a firecracker went off. I immediately hit the ground. July 2 was not the ideal day to come back from a war zone. I knew this reaction was going to be something that had to be controlled but in the next few days it was going to be difficult. I decided to just stick around the house until after the fourth of July.

The next evening I was watching television when a good friend came in. He was with his girlfriend, another couple and a single girl. I thought, "Damn, he got me a date." The last thing I wanted to do was go on a date. Then a few more people came in. My mother was throwing me a surprise party. She told me that she invited twenty-five or thirty people but before you knew it there were well over a hundred people there. You throw a good party and the whole neighborhood comes out. It felt good seeing everybody.

I was outside talking to a couple of friends when a firecracker went off. Down I went. I came up smiling. The guys were breaking my chops, we were all laughing. I overheard one of the girls ask another if she thought I was shell-shocked. I wanted to explain to her that the reaction to that sound was something that kept me alive just a couple of days ago. It was just a reflex and there was nothing wrong with me but how do you say that? Even if you weren't in Vietnam people look at you strange when you go around telling them that you are not crazy. A couple of the other guys noticed my reaction and went around asking people not to shoot off fireworks, including the kids on the block. They stopped. I wanted to explain that the fireworks did not bother me; it was just a reaction that I had to get under control. I knew that I was home and not in the war, but that's tough to explain. Rather than making an issue out of it you keep quiet. The party lasted all night and I had a great time.

I knew that I had been through the war but I didn't think that I was any different. The firecracker incident made me realize that people's perception of you is different but I was basically the same or so I thought.

The unwritten law is that you do not talk about combat experiences. Probably because you're supposed to forget, which is impossible, or you will be perceived as a person who is bragging or disturbed. Personally I really didn't want to talk about it but that leaves a void. People talk about what they experienced. If you talk to a teacher, at some point it will usually be about teaching, a nurse, a cop, a lawyer, a fire fighter, whoever. Their personal job experience will usually come into the conversation. My job was that of a soldier but if you were looking not to bring that into conversations, your communication with people can become limited. It wasn't a big problem for me but I could see how it could be.

I started to realize that not only didn't I want to talk about the war with non-veterans but if you did they really couldn't understand.

I was sitting in a bar, still home on leave, when I over heard a conversation. That day there was a report that eight members of the 82nd had been killed. Apparently they had been sleeping on guard. They weren't from my company but I felt a deep sorrow when I heard it. The people at the bar were mocking them. What types of soldiers were they? They deserved to be dead if they were sleeping on guard. No wonder why we are not winning this war. They kept it up. I do not think that they realized that I was from the 82nd or that I was there. I was getting angry, luckily I was sober. I just wanted to get up and punch them, but I didn't. They weren't talking directly to me so I just couldn't get up and punch them. I was going to get into the conversation but I realized they just wouldn't understand. After all, you shouldn't be sleeping on guard but it happens. I yelled down, "Change the conversation." They looked at me, I knew a couple of them. One guy continued. I stood up and said it one more time, "Change the conversation." They stopped. I sat down and started thinking. Nobody should sleep on guard but I remember times when that was easier said than done. You could be so tired, you might have been humping the bush for days with relatively little sleep at night, that you became exhausted. I used to use little gimmicks to stay awake. I always made sure that I had extra water so that I could drink it while on guard. That would usually refresh you. For a while I would brush my teeth but they made me stop because it made too much noise. I always inverted me helmet and sat on it. That way if you tended to doze off the shifting of your weight would cause a falling sensation that would snap you awake.

I woke up one night and looked over towards the guard position. The person on guard, I'll call him Sergeant D, was struggling to stay awake. Sergeant D was an instant N.C.O. who arrived in country a couple of weeks prior to myself. He was a soft spoken, good natured, highly moral person. He was an excellent leader who was bright, considerate, would take charge and there was never a qualm about following his decisions. At times he was our platoon leader, an officer's position, and was one of the few draftees who served two years and left the army with a rank of E6, that's one step above a three stripe sergeant, and he deserved it.

As I lay there watching him, he was sitting down and his head was starting to nod. He stood up, struggling to stay awake. He put his rifle butt on the ground, using it for support. Then he literally fell asleep standing on his feet. I looked over to the other guard position, he was awake but did not notice Sergeant D. I watched the sarge, he must have been sleeping for about two minutes when a shift in his body weight caused him to start falling. He caught himself, snapping awake. Sergeant D was one of the best soldiers that I had served with and if he could fall asleep on guard, anyone was capable of falling asleep.

The squad from the 82nd was probably out on ambush and set up in one eight-man position. We used to set up that way up north but you would run into the problem of someone falling asleep. We changed, if you were in a squad sized ambush we would set up in two positions, thereby having two people on guard thus eliminating the sleep factor. I do not know what happened when that squad was killed but the people at the bar should have been mourning their death but instead were mocking them. I could understand where they were coming from although it was upsetting me but I also knew they could never understand it from the Veteran's position. I had a couple of more beers and then left.

You start to realize that not only are people's perceptions of you are different but that you are different. That reality did not come to me all at once but as time went on you came to that realization. In fact I am still dealing with it.

My leave was over and it was back to do my last six months in the army. Congressman Emanuel Cellars had my orders changed so that I was to be stationed at Fort Meade, Maryland. The closest he could get me to home. As they were processing me in, the person from personnel was from Brooklyn. He looked at my scores then asked me if I'd be interested in a job in personnel. The alternative was to be assigned to an infantry unit that was practicing war games. I jumped at the chance. The fact that the army assigned you to a unit that played war games created many problems. You could understand if they assigned you to train recruits who were about to go to Vietnam but that was usually reserved for people who had at least a year left on their hitch. Most veterans were just looking to get out but the army wouldn't do that, with the exception of early discharges to attend college, they made you stick out the two years. They placed people in these training units that were regular army. Spit and polish and chicken shit. The returning Veterans attitude was incompatible for this life style. These were draftees not volunteers. They had to ask themselves, what the hell were they training for? They did their time, they weren't going back. They became subjected to the menial tasks that only the military could come up with, probably taking orders about combat training from people that were never there. It's hard to put up with that type of bullshit after you experienced a war.

There were a lot of Vietnam veterans who received discharges other than honorable. Not because of what they did in Vietnam but because of what they were subjected to by the military in their remaining months of service. The military did not know what to do with these Veterans. There was no place for them. They just should have let them go, tell them, job well done and give them their honorable discharge. I was very lucky to be assigned to personnel because I know that I wouldn't have put up with their chicken shit.

I continued to work in personnel but I started to get very tired. I came home one weekend and did not get out of bed the whole time. I went back to the army but I couldn't get up for reveille. I went to the hospital and they did some tests. I was sitting in the waiting room when a doctor came out calling my name. I started to get up but he told me to sit there. He told the medics to get a stretcher. He said that my white blood cell count was so high that he didn't know how I was conscious. They kept me in the hospital for five or six weeks. They were constantly testing me, taking blood a couple of times a day. They would not tell me what was wrong. They told me that I had contracted infectious hepatitis but there was a lot more to the problem than that. For a while they thought I might have a type of leukemia but thankfully that turned out to be negative. They did not know what was wrong and they couldn't keep my white blood cells under control. I felt weak and tired. I must have slept twenty hours out of the day. That lasted four or five weeks then I started to regain some strength. The white blood count came down but was still high. I started to become restless and wanted out of the hospital. The doctors just kept testing me saying that the white blood count was still too high but they did not know why. I was feeling better and wanted out of the hospital. Finally, they sent me home for a seven-day convalescent leave. I just stayed around the house but I was up most of the time, eating, watching television, talking to friends, that type of thing. When I went back they put me back in the hospital. The white blood count was a little better but still too high. They kept me there for about a week, more testing, but they could not figure out what was wrong. The doctors said that they tried everything that they could think of but my white blood count just would not return to normal. They decided to send me home for a thirty-day convalescent leave. I was happy. They gave me a list of things to do and not to do. No medication. One of the things was not to drink alcohol. I told the doctor that I felt good. You are sending me home for thirty days, I know I am going to have a couple of beers with friends. He said you should not drink but if you do, drink red wine, it might be good for your blood. During those thirty days I ate well and drank a lot of red wine, for medicinal purposes of course.

I started hanging out with a bunch of guys from the neighborhood, all recent Vietnam Veterans. There were about a dozen or so of us. We drank, got high and talked politics. We all wanted the war to end although not necessarily for the same reasons. There was an anti-war rally in Washington D.C. in November of 1969. We all decided to go. We drove down in one guy's Volkswagen bus. It was more like a party than anything else. Coincidentally it coincided with the end of my convalescent leave. When the demonstration was over they drove me back to the base. The guard stopped us at the gate. I explained that I was coming back from leave and they were just dropping me off. He looked bewildered but let us pass. It was some sight, about a dozen long haired hippy looking Vietnam Vets invading an army base. I showed them around and people were staring, we all had a good laugh.

Then it was back to the hospital. They ran some more tests and told me everything was all right. My white blood count was normal and I was in perfect health. I asked a lot of questions but they had no answers. Whatever it was you had it is now gone. If you feel weak or tired come back. Then they released me to my unit.

In thinking back there was not one time that they ever mentioned Agent Orange. I was in plenty of areas that had been defoliated but they never asked. At the time I did not know what Agent Orange was. I do not think that Agent Orange had anything to do with what was wrong with me, but who knows? They didn't let me know that it was a possibility. That's a disgrace. I risked my life for this country and now my health was in jeopardy but they would not inform me about the possible cause. It could make you bitter.

It reoccurred twice in the last twenty odd years. I asked some doctors about it but they did not know. I think it left me with an overactive immune system that kicks in when infections enter my body but I am just guessing. I was going to go to the V.A. to be examined but it's very difficult for me to trust them. Hopefully it will not reoccur again.

When I went back to my job at personnel it was taken. They sent me back to headquarters. The first sergeant told me that I was assigned to Headquarters company. The only problem, if you want to call it that, was that they didn't assign me to any particular job. There was nobody that I had to report to. The only thing was that my name came up on duty roster every couple of weeks. Headquarters company did not even have a roll call in the morning.

The first couple of days I hung around, went to the movies, the P.X. But it got boring. Finally I just went home. I came back a couple of days later and nobody missed me. I checked the duty roster, my name was not there, so I stopped by to see top. We had a brief discussion about how he was once at Coney Island and how he hated it. He did not say anything else so I left. I went over to personnel, talked to a couple of people, they told me that I was being marked present on the morning report, so I got hold of this photographer who was a buddy, gave him my home phone number and asked him to call if anything came up. Then I went home. I would go back once a week or so, go through the rounds making sure everything was all right. Then go home again. My parents used to question me, telling me it was stupid to mess up now that it was so close to my discharge. My father was an officer and a former M.P. I told him how I had everything covered. He said that it sounds like you do but what happens if you get into an accident while you are here. I did not think of that but I decided to take my chances. Nothing happened, that is until New Year's Eve. I received a call from my buddy a couple of days prior telling me that I was on K.P. New Year's Eve. I was going to go back but I remembered how I spent last New Year's so I stayed for the party. I went back late New Year's Day and slept in my bunk for the rest of the night. In the morning a message came that top wanted me in his office. He was pissed.

"Where were you New Year's Eve?"

"I was here."

"You were supposed to be on K.P. Do not give me any bull. Where were you?" "I was here. I just must have missed my name on the duty roster." We both knew that he had messed up by not assigning me to a particular job. He said that he was going to give me an article 15 for missing duty. I left his office figuring that it was a small price to pay for being home on New Year's Eve.

An article 15 is an in house punishment that can range anywhere from a reprimand to a loss of rank and pay. A couple of days later he handed me the article 15. Punishment was three days "extra duty" and a small loss in pay. Then I noticed that he had down the wrong dates. They give you 48 hours to sign it or protest it. I was going to sign it because I did not want to break top's chops. He was not a bad guy but I could not resist. I waited for forty-eight hours then put a protest in with the captain. I showed him the duty roster for the date that was stated in the article 15 and that I was not assigned duty for the day. He dismissed the article 15. The next day top called me into his office, he was fuming. He yelled at me for about five minutes then asked me what I had to say. I told him to calm down and relax and stop taking things so personally. He just stared. By that time I did not even feel like I was in the army. I just talked to him man to man. We wound up talking for about a half-hour. It became friendly but he told me he was going to re-issue the article 15. They gave it to me and I signed it. I did the three days "extra duty" but somehow the orders to take the money were lost between personnel and finance.

It became time for me to start processing out. They put you through whole procedure. You had to turn in your equipment but most of mine was stolen while I was in the hospital. They wanted me to pay for it so I wound up doctoring the form. There was one last thing that I had to complete. They made you talk to the reenlistment officer. It was some young second lieutenant who had to break my chops. I explained to him that the army wasn't for me but he would not sign my form. He made me come back the next day. The next day he gave me a harder time. We were alone. I told him that he was not going to get his bonus from my ass, just stop breaking my balls and sign the paper.

"You can't talk to me that way."

I started getting angry. I thought about physically threatening him but instead I told him that I was going to put a complaint in against him that would make their heads spin. That I would create a large blemish on his career and very softly told him to just sign the paper. He thought for a second and signed the paper.

The attitude that had developed in Vietnam about not taking bullshit from everyone had stayed with me. In fact it was evolving to a higher level. I was aware of it but it didn't seem to matter. Was I lucky that I was not assigned to a training unit?

It was my last day. They gave me my separation papers and asked me to read them to make sure that everything was correct. I looked them over and noticed that my army accommodation medal and Bronze Star were not there. They said that they did not have orders for them. I thought for a second and realized they were probably sitting in Fort Benning, Georgia. It really was not that important to me. Besides they said that they could be amended so I let it go. They handed me my separation papers. I went to finance to pick up my money and I was out of the army.

On the ride home I was thinking about everything. I served honorably in Vietnam and my obligation to my country was fulfilled. I was glad that I was out of the service but I was also proud to have served. Now on with the rest of my life.

The Vietnam Veteran

There are millions of stories that could be told about Vietnam. I just related some of my experiences in order to give you a flavor and somewhat of an understanding of what it was like to be there and to a degree the effect these experiences had upon me. Unfortunately it is difficult to understand what the actual effects are and how much they influence you as a person.

To try to explain the Vietnam Veteran as a monolithic entity is an unrealistic endeavor. We were all different in our experiences and our actions both while we were there and in our subsequent life thereafter. What I will try to do is explore some common themes that are applicable to all of us, some of us, or just a few of us, using my own perceptions and experiences in order to try to understand this animal we call the Vietnam Veteran.

The Vietnam Veteran is portrayed as being different from veterans of other wars and in many ways this is true. All soldiers returning from war had to readjust but for the Vietnam Veteran there were just many more variables. Take something as simple as being transported back from the war. I don't know if the veterans of other wars had counseling or debriefing or anything of that nature but I know that they had something that was even better. That is, an unsupervised form of group therapy. They spent at least a month traveling together aboard ship before they arrived home. Most of the time was probably spent talking about their hopes and their dreams, but there had to be some time for reflection and understanding of what they had just experienced. I am sure, if they saw a buddy was having a problem, they would spend time talking it out with him. Just the mere fact that they had a month to adjust between the war and their arrival home had to go a long way in easing their readjustment into society and for most it was a lot longer than a month between the time that their war ended and their arrival home. This was not true for all problems but it had to help immensely in many areas.

I was home in my house and less than a week prior I had been under mortar attack. I left the war zone oneday and because of the time differentials I was home that same day. There was no counseling, no debriefing. Nobody to even tell you what to expect. You could have immediate problems, latent problems, and inevitablly you were going to have adjustment problems but nobody made you aware of any of this. They should have landed you in Hawaii or somewhere and kept you there for at least two weeks. During that time there should have been counseling or debriefing and maybe a little good old unsupervised group therapy. We all would have bitched because we wanted to go home but it would have gone a long way in easing our readjustment to society.

The military had billions to spend to send you to a place that would tear your life apart but when it came time to help you put it back together they were non-existent.

The readjustment and acceptance which was supposed to have an integrative effect between us and society in reality tended to foster the segregation of the Vietnam Veteran.

Outside of the family the place that you would expect to be most accepted was the traditional Veterans' organizations such as the American Legion, the Veterans of Foreign Wars, and other such organizations, but this turned out not to be the case. These organizations were comprised mainly of World War II and Korean Veterans. The Korean Veterans, when they returned had to go through a readjustment and acceptance of their own. The chauvinistic attitude of the World War II Veteran created a division. They treated the Korean Veteran like a second class citizen. Their attitude was that we fought in the big war, you guys don't know what war was is all about. You didn't even fight in a war. You were engaged in a police action. This left the Korean Veteran in a position where they thought they had to defend themselves.

Any person who has been in combat knows that a war, a conflict, a police action is merely a matter of semantics. Combat is combat regardless of what you want to title the particular entity in which it took place.

This left a bitter taste in the mouths of the Korean Veteran and they are still fighting for recognition but otherwise their acceptance was tolerable. This argument of "I fought in a real war" to a lesser degree continues today and probably will raise its head again, with a different flavor and perhaps a little more credence, when the Dessert Storm Veteran assimilates and the hoopla from that war dies down.

When the Vietnam Veteran started entering these organizations there were a multitude of factors that contributed to his alienation. The "I fought in the real war" syndrome was sort of played out but there were many other factors. The greatest of these was the times and change that society in general was going through. The anti-war, anti-establishment, peace and drug sub-culture was now manifesting itself as the predominant acceptance for the youth of America.

This created many problems for the Vietnam Veteran. If you joined one of the Veterans organizations there was an immediate conflict of a generation gap. This became most apparent if you attended a social. They were into ballroom dancing, Guy Lombardo, and liquor. While we might drink, we were into rock-n-roll, smoking pot, and doing our own thing. This was not the only thing that divided us. They had an agenda, which we felt did not address our concerns. There were problems peculiar to us, Agent Orange just being one example, that weren't being addressed properly. The alienation became so strong that we did not feel like we belonged so people either dropped out or started their own organizations. People need to feel accepted. These organizations did not provide that.

You also look for acceptance among your peers. There was a whole social evolution going on that was causing problems and moral dilemmas among the youth in general. You had your own problems and moral dilemmas to deal with which might not coincide with the flow of the times.

It is easy for a veteran, especially a combat veteran, to be anti-war. No one should have to experience the death and destruction and traumatic effects that a war brings upon an individual. To become part of the anti-war movement was a natural occurrence but even though we seemed to have the same ultimate goal, whether or not there was a mutual acceptance is a different story.

The more you got to know the males in the anti-war movement the more you started wondering about their motives. They were expressing moral platitudes about our involvement in the war and the rhetoric of the peace movement but in essence you started to realize that a lot of them were just afraid to go. You began to feel that you knew the reasons why you were against the war but the integrity of the motives of some of the people in the peace movement might have been self-motivated. Then although you understood the realities of war you started to feel that the moral philosophies that you were hearing were really self-indulging. You started to have the attitude that degenerated to a level of, "who do these people think they are?" I was put in a position that I had to put my life on the line, but your life is too good to be put on the line?

There were many sincere people with high moral integrity who were part of the peace movement but I came to the reality that most of the people, especially the males, were just full of shit. Where was the moral outrage, the indignation, the peace movement rhetoric, when millions upon millions of people in Cambodia were slaughtered? It did not affect these individuals in their personal lives so their high moral philosophies became superfluous.

There were other segments of the anti-war movement characterized by people like Jane Fonda. She went over to North Vietnam, consorted with the enemy, had her picture taken straddled upon an artillery piece, a phallic symbol that could be interpreted as "Fuck the G.I.'s." Then she made anti-American propaganda that was heard by the POW's and American soldiers.

It caused such harm and such pain that she should have been tried for treason. I could not be part of that element of the anti-war movement.

The people in general were against the war but they could not distinguish between the war and the people who fought in the war. The more radical elements would call us murderers and baby killers. Most of us would reply that we were not murderers or baby killers. Some, who were going through a lot of soul searching, were affected deeply by these actions.

The anti-war movement seemed like the natural place for acceptance but in reality with all the complexities involved it tended to further alienate some of us, although there were veterans who found a home there. Mostly, however, the anti-war veterans found a mutual unacceptability and formed their own association. The Vietnam Veterans Against War.

Personally I was against the war not only because of the needless loss of life but also because of the political realities. The government was merely conducting an exercise over there, using us as the guinea pigs. The goal of winning the war was not a political imperative. I initially became involved with the anti-war movement but became disillusioned with some of the people involved. I wanted the war to end but I could not reconcile in my mind whether the anti-war movement was helping to attain that goal or to further complicate it. How it affected the troops who were still fighting many years after my return was a problem for me. I am still not sure if the anti-war movement helped to end the war or prolong it because of the political indecisiveness it created.

The family was the natural place for acceptance but for some even this presented problems. There were parents that could not accept that their little boy was now a man. Thereby, not giving the space and the freedom that was needed for proper psychological development.

As Vietnam Veterans we did not fully understand the pain and the suffering that our families went through because of our being in Vietnam.

The typical married man who was eventually confronted by his wife about what she went though, he could not equate in his mind the seriousness and importance of her tribulations compared to what he had just experienced, probably causing both to have a lack of acceptance for each other.

In my case my family was my strong point. My parents gave me the love and understanding and the space I needed as an individual. My mother, whom I had conflicts with prior to Vietnam, gave me the acceptance that I needed. My older brother, who had just completed his masters' degree, was himself drafted into the service and was in Okinawa when I came home. My two sisters were both in college and they had experienced a form of alienation from their peers because I was in Vietnam. My younger brother was just starting high school and he had to face the prospect that he might eventually get drafted. Collectively they gave me the support and respect that I needed to feel accepted.

My father, who was my friend, gave me the ultimate acceptance. As a twenty-one year old person he respected me as a man. My family gave me all the strength that I needed for my acceptance back into society. That does not mean that I did not face problems but they were easier to deal with because of this.

Acceptability is a difficult concept to fathom at times, it is the individual's perceptions that dictate whether or not he is being accepted. There were probably numerous occasions when the Vietnam Veteran felt that he was not being accepted, where in reality that might not have been the case. In my college days I felt alienated and formed very few associations there but back in the neighborhood there was an automatic acceptance. People were people. Whether you were a veteran or a draft dodger, we all seemed to come together.

There was a loose knit group of us, all Vietnam Veterans, who would occasionally gather together. There was a brotherhood there. We rarely talked about our experiences in the war but we did talk politics. There was a basic consensus that we knew that we had been used and an overwhelming attitude that wanted change and an end to the war. We probably did each other more good than we realized at the time. Within a year or so we all went our separate ways but I am glad that the association was there for me while it existed.

The feeling that there was no place for us except among ourselves, whether it was real or just perceived, became a major problem for many Vietnam Veterans.

The quest for acceptance for too many Vietnam Veterans wound up in the drug culture. If you did drugs, no matter what your background, you were automatically accepted in the group. Drugs back then were looked at in a different light. The consequences of drug abuse, with exception of maybe heroin, were not understood or even have thought to be a threat. For the Vietnam Veteran perhaps more so. Most of us had experimented with at least marijuana and believed that there was not much harm in using drugs. The military, in its own way, helped foster that belief because they did absolutely nothing to educate us or make us aware of the dangers of drugs. In fact the Veterans Administration was a main supplier of drugs. There were many people who were going through emotional or readjustment problems who went to the VA for counseling and wound up being put on one type of barbiturate or another. I know veterans who never took drugs in their lives who wound up being addicted to pills because of the policies of the VA.

The drug culture was an easy comrade for the Vietnam Veteran. The fact that it allowed a form of escapism, which many veterans desired, they wanted to forget what they just experienced. The acceptance and having associates with whom you had a common experience, drugs, was appealing. Unfortunately when the inevitable problems of using drugs started to arise many veterans could not find their way out.

As for myself my first year or so I experimented with a myriad of drugs falling susceptible to none with the exception of marijuana. I smoked too much pot for too many years. Although I do not think that there were any long-term effects and the relief from stress was welcome, I know that I am much better off without it. I have not smoked pot with any regularity for years.

Another problem for the Vietnam Vet was that of attitude. Both the attitude he acquired towards society and the perception of that attitude by society toward the Vietnam Vet. There were many variables that affected that attitude and many different attitudes that emerged.

Dealing with authority could become a problem, especially for the combat veteran. The fact that you were placed in a combat situation you developed independence, almost a freedom that had you look at authority in a unique way. Authority was no longer a dictator. You respected authority only when you felt that the authority deserved respect. In actual combat there was an automatic control because you knew that you had to blindly respect the orders that were given. In civilian life this control did not exist. You had to have the control and discipline within yourself and form judgments about what authority you were going to deem as deserving respect. Your automatic acceptance of authority was no longer part of your nature. Partly do to the fact that you could not be automatically submissive to authority. Therefore, you had to make your own judgments in many situations. Sometimes there were errors in the judgment that you made.

A veteran who returned to his job and had to take orders from someone that he felt had nowhere near his life experiences, could become apprehensive or even defiant of that person's authority. This was an error in judgment that created many conflicts. You had to relearn that it was not the person but the position they held that emanated the authority. You would think that being in the military this would be automatic but somehow you were left with the opposite approach. Probably because of all the authority that you had to succumb to in basic training and when you acquired this newfound independence and freedom in your dealings in Vietnam, you started seeing the person that was telling you what to do. You were on a man to man level. If you did not like what he was saying or doing you would let him know. The only way that they could exercise their authority, if your defiant, was to court martial you and that option was greatly watered down because the punishment in essence was better than being in the field. So because of the circumstances involved there was an evolution to near equality among soldiers in the field. Everyone still had their position so there was still an order and chain of command but the questioning of a person who was in authority was just that, the questioning of a person, not necessarily his authority. You tended to transcend the authority and deal with the person.

When you brought this same attitude back to the States it brought you trouble. The questioning of the person in authority in the military was not acceptable. If defiant their recourse could lead to a court martial or dishonorable discharge. Too many veterans had the attitude that because that they were combat veterans certain types of authority should not apply to them. In some cases this evolved to an outright disrespect for authority.

Freedom is sometimes difficult to handle because freedom without the necessary discipline to limit that freedom to conform to the natural order of your surroundings could lead to disaster. Most combat veterans experienced a certain kind of freedom with regard to authority but if you did not learn to control that freedom to conform to your new environment you could get eaten up by that authority. Because we have experienced this type of freedom we will always be susceptible to defiance. Our job now is to be able to judge when that defiance is warranted. It would be easy to adhere to authority, just because that authority exists, but for combat veterans that is impossible. We must make our own judgments with regard to authority but unfortunately they might not always be correct.

The questioning of authority sometimes led you in the right direction. Take the Agent Orange conflict. There were many veterans coming down with various medical problems, especially certain forms of cancer, that were abnormally high compared to the general population. The veterans looked for causes, which pointed to the chemical dioxin that was found in Agent Orange, a defoliant used extensively in Vietnam. The government, in spite of the fact that it stopped using it, issued statements that there was no correlation between the use of dioxins and the illnesses that were occurring. If the veterans accepted the authority of the government and did not question the credence of these statements, it would have been left at that, but fortunately this was not the situation. Through much research and many lawsuits the veterans have won a mild victory. There is still much more work to be done in this area.

In dealing with the P.O.W. and M.I.A.'s the veterans again have to defy the authority of the government because their stance is that they do not exist. We know that this is purely political because the government has reneged on war reparations, besides that, there have been just too many sightings for us not to question their existence. The government has been engaged in a cover up, which is now starting to come to light. They set up many phony commissions to deal with this problem but the latest one is being exposed by the officer who was in charge of it. There is a long way to go, if ever, before the truth wins out but I know in my heart that there are still veterans held in Southeast Asia. I could have been one of them, aside from what my ordeal would have been, could you imagine the pain and suffering that it would have caused my family? I wish the government would just eat its pride, reverse its policy, and do everything they can to bring those veterans home but the political implications might be too strong. Because of these factors and many others the Vietnam Veteran developed attitudes of defiance and anger, to that of lack of respect for our government.

Most people believe that because you served in Vietnam that the government paid for your college education. When I first went to college in 1970 the government paid me one hundred and thirty five dollars per month under the G.I. bill. While it was better than nothing it nowhere near covered the tuition and expenses at most colleges, no less living expenses. This gradually increased because the veterans fought for it but it was still nowhere near adequate.

After World War II they had something called the 52-20 club, which entitled them to twenty dollars a week for fifty-two weeks. We were put on unemployment. Just a connotation of being on unemployment created an aura of non-recognition. I received fifty-two dollars a week but I could not collect it if I went to school.

They replaced my teeth, which had been knocked out but this was only a one shot deal. If my bridge broke, which has happened, the government will not pay for it.

The general public probably feels that the G.I. bill provided many benefits for the Vietnam Veteran but in reality there were few. There were no benefits that I could have received that I would not have been entitled to if I spent the whole time in Hawaii or anywhere else. There were no set asides that were specifically designed for the veterans who served in Vietnam. Recently the federal and some local governments have designated certain programs exclusively for the Vietnam Veteran. While appreciated it's more like the case of too little too late.

The recognition or lack of it began to affect your attitude. You felt that you were used and abused and now just cast aside. That created quite a furor, which caused many veterans to complain about the treatment that they were receiving. Some of the people in the general public accused us of being crybabies. That also did wonders for your attitude.

The Vietnam War not only affected the Veteran; it also had a profound impact on society. There were as many variations of thought and attitude by the general public as there were by the veterans themselves.

The lack of government recognition was not unique to the Vietnam Veteran, after WWI the veterans thought they were entitled to a bonus. I am not sure if the government reneged or the Veterans misunderstood but they marched on Washington demanding payment. They set up shanty towns. The government eventually brought out the military to chase them out of Washington.

Another aspect of your attitude can be described by the engraving on a cigarette lighter I picked up in Vietnam. There was a picture of "Snoopy" lying down on top of his doghouse. In the cartoon like bubble there were the words "Fuck It." That became the attitude of many veterans. You just did not care. A lot of things just did not seem important. At times I had this attitude especially if I was drinking.

Alcohol was a substance that affected many veterans in various ways. Some would drink to try to forget, some for the excitement, others would turn to alcohol because of emotional or readjustment problems they were experiencing. For me alcohol was different. In a sense it was part of the Irish American culture. While I never drank at home and usually would not let it interfere with what I had to do, there was rarely a time when I was out socializing when alcohol was not part of it. This usually was not a problem but there were times when I would just out and out abuse it. This would happen because of the attitude I had at the moment. I just did not care. Fuck it. Nothing seemed to matter. I would go out on a two-day drunk, it would be an adventure, an experience and I did not care what happened. It caused some problems and would create enemies out of friends but it was basically a release of frustrations. The only time I would talk about Vietnam was while I was out on one of these drunks. There was a time for many years, except for St. Patrick's Day, when these drinking bouts did not occur but while writing this book they have occurred too frequently.

Another reason why alcohol and drugs became part of the Veteran's post-war experience was because you developed a yearning for excitement. Not necessarily a living on the edge type of syndrome, which did exist for some, but because of the war you just were not ready for a mundane type of existence.

There was a song that I believe came out after WWI which was titled "How do you keep them down on the farm after they've seen Paree." I don't remember all of the lyrics but the message was that after a person has been exposed to the excitement and diversities that a city like Paris has to offer, you can't expect them to go back to the farm and be content with just plowing the fields. Once you are exposed to a type of experience, which generates excitement it is difficult to take that excitement factor out of your life.

War if nothing else generates an excitement. It is not your ordinary, everyday, run of the mill type of existence. The adjustment that is required to return to that type of existence is not an easy transition. You feel that there is more to life. Your senses, the excitement factor, have been titillated. You look to sow your wild oats but life does not always allow for this, thereby causing frustration that can become overwhelming.

The veteran who returned to a mundane job in a factory or an office could become frustrated without actually realizing why. They just knew that there was not a satisfaction in what they were presently experiencing.

There was also a strong correlation between this excitement factor and the veteran's personal relationships. Many marriages and relationships suffered because the veteran was trying to satisfy this excitement factor, thereby alienating their loved ones.

The times that were allowing for a new type of permissiveness were also a great factor. The sexual revolution, drug culture, anti-establishment, non-conformist, do your own thing way of life, was an existence that many veterans were drawn to because of this need to satisfy the excitement factor. Rather than try to control this excitement factor and readjust they would exploit it in this newfound cultural changes that society was experiencing.

For veterans of any war there is a period of time that is needed in order readjust, to control what needs to be controlled, to put things in the proper perspective that would allow you to normalize your life and understand the values of society that must be adhered to in order to lead a so-called normal life. The problem for the Vietnam Veteran was that there was no constant. The values of society, although many were temporary, were in transition. The Veteran themselves were in a different type of transition. So when they had to come to grips with values that were askew because of the war, it became a very complex adjustment. When dealing with religion, authority, war, life, death, race, drugs, sex, relationships, work ethic, lifestyle, conformity and the moral connotations that can be associated with these concepts the veteran had to form his own understanding. This became complicated. Unlike other veterans who had to reevaluate their moral positions the Vietnam Veteran had many other variables with which they had to deal. Other veterans who had moral dilemmas had a constant. There were basic moral values that were intrinsic to society at large. They would then work out their understanding by using these intrinsic values as a guide in which to compare their dilemma.

The Vietnam Veteran in forming his understanding, when looking for guidance, saw the same intrinsic values but also saw them in upheaval. Their comparisons became many and unfortunately the judgments that they ascertained in many instances led them down the wrong path. As I stated previously, it is much easier to believe in something that appears to be fundamentally right, because you were taught it was that way, than to question the fundamental integrity of something and form your own beliefs. The Vietnam Veteran was now questioning both the fundamental integrity of the basic values that had been intrinsic to society at large and the newly formed values that were pervading society.

The typical veteran was immediately faced with the question of whether or not the war that he had just participated in was a moral war. This was a debate that was flourishing throughout the country. The debate ran the gamut from no war is moral to my country right or wrong. This was academic to most people but to the veteran it was very real. My country right or wrong was a hard pill to swallow because the veteran already experienced their government in a wrongful situation, that is, the strategy used in fighting the war which needlessly caused thousands upon thousands of American soldiers to be killed or wounded. You were already questioning the strategy, to question our involvement was an easy next step. The multitude of questions that arose from that and the seemingly lack of adequate answers became perplexing. The traditional institutions such as government and religion were themselves fending off so many questions because of the cultural changes that any answers coming from them became suspect. If you started to believe that our involvement was not morally correct then was the taking of the lives of other soldiers and perhaps civilians actually murder? The pat answer that you were involved in a war and just following orders was the same answer that was used to justify the atrocities that were perpetuated during the Holocaust. This caused deep soul searching for many veterans who were without satisfactory answers.

This was only one of many moral questions that were coming to light. To what extent was race a factor? Was communism the evil that we were led to believe? While dealing with these and other moral problems the veteran was also being tugged at by the problems of acceptance, authority, the anti-war movement, drugs, alcohol, social changes, and to some their emotional dealings with fear and traumatic experiences. There was a lot happening with few answers. So when someone like Timothy Leary said to turn on, tune in and drop out, it became an attractive path for some veterans. Back to nature, living in a commune or the myriad of new religions and guru philosophies were paths that some took to find answers. Some banded together with other Vietnam Veterans looking for answers. This tended to cause self-segregation. Then some became alienated from everything, a loner.

The readjustment back to mainstream America became a long and winding road with many tributaries, which caused many veterans not to reach their final destination.

Not all Vietnam Veterans were affected by all of the problems that I discussed but to one degree or another some of these problems affected all of us. There is one thing that affected everyone who spent time in Vietnam. That is fear.

When you think of fear you might assume that the combat veteran would be most affected but I am not sure that this is the case. In any war it takes five to six military personnel for every infantry soldier in the field. Not every infantry soldier saw actual combat. So the number of people who actually saw combat is a small percentage of the people who served in Vietnam, yet fear was a factor for everyone.

Just because you were not infantry did not mean you did not experience a war. There were no so-called front lines. All of Vietnam was a war zone. Some areas much worse then others but you were susceptible to a mortar or rocket attack or a type of terrorism even in the safer areas.

Everyone experienced fear. Fear is a strange thing, it can grow on you. If you were a non-infantry soldier who came under mortar or rocket attack, that would bring you to a higher level of fear but you would have no release or reaction toward the enemy that created it. The fear could continue to grow even after the attack stopped. You experienced fear but you did not know what your reactions would be if it was a combat situation. You knew that you were scared and that fear could play in your mind. It could create self-doubts to wonder if you are man enough to deal with it if you actually had to fight the enemy. You did not get the opportunity to know your reactions so this frightening situation could create a fear that just festered in your mind. It could lead to emotional problems that could be with you for life. Even if you were never under attack just being in a war zone could create a fear that grew on you that could be out of proportion with reality. This could cause similar types of emotional problems.

The combat veteran knows his reaction in his dealings with fear. For some the fear took control, probably causing numerous emotional problems that will never go away. For most, however, they experienced the fear and reacted in the proper manner. Fear did not take control. You transcended the fear so it did not impair your reactions and at times combat gave you a release from fear because of this transcendence. Fear would come back and there would be other situations where you had to deal with it again but you dealt with it. You knew fear was not going to control your reactions. There was no self-doubt. In essence you conquered your fear of fear. While there were many emotional problems unique to the combat veteran fear, at least for the majority, fear was not one of them because you knew you could deal with it.

In civilian life this helped me on a number of occasions and probably saved my life in one. A friend and I were coming back from a Giants football game. We were drinking and made a few stops. We were driving home when our car stalled in downtown Brooklyn at Atlantic and Flatbush Avenues. It was about ten p.m. This had happened before and we could either jump-start the car or after about a half-hour it would start. I did not feel like waiting. There was a carnival in a parking lot right on the corner so I went in to see if anyone had jumper cables and would help us. An argument ensued with one of the carnival workers over a cigarette. My friend came in looking for me. He was a big man, about six-two and better than two hundred and fifty pounds. The carnival worker felt endangered and reached down towards his ankle. I saw a gun. My friend and I took off. We got outside and turned around and there were fifteen to twenty carnival workers in pursuit. They each had something in their hands, a bat, club, sticks, chains or something. They surrounded us. My friend was about ten yards from me. Then I was hit over the head with an ax handle, in the back with a sledgehammer. I was trying to fend them off but blood was rushing down my face. Then for a moment everything stopped. I guess they could not believe I was still on my feet. I knew if I went down it was all over. I used that moment to go towards my friend. He was fending off his own attackers. We had to get out of there so I grabbed him by the shirt and pulled him out into the oncoming traffic. There was screeching of brakes and honking of horns but luckily most were slowing down to watch what was happening. We got into the middle of the street and there was a taxi. He stopped, we jumped in, and he took us to a police station. I wound up with multiple stitches in my head and bruises all over my body. My friend had a broken arm and multiple bruises. We were fortunate. We also gave the cab driver a nice tip.

As unlikely as this might sound there was no fear in me once they started attacking. When I saw the gun, while we were running, there was a fear. Once the physical contact started I transcended that fear. An automatic reaction that allowed me to think clearly with reguard to defending myself and to look for an escape route. My friend, who reacted properly, probably did not have the automatic reaction that allowed his mind to be free from fear. He had another variable to contend with in a situation that called for split second reactions. My friend, who knows he reacted properly in a fearful situation, will probably develop this ability to transcend fear because he has already experienced his reaction in a life and death situation.

Do not misunderstand. Combat did not leave me fearless. In a sense because you experienced such degrees of fear it makes you more susceptible. If a ninety-eight pound weakling challenges me a degree of fear will run through me. If a two hundred and ninety-eight-pound strongman challenges me a proportionately higher degree of fear will run through me. What combat did was allow me to react to the situation without fear being a factor. It is initially there but you transcend it.

Veterans without combat experience, experienced fear to one degree or another. Depending on the degree of mental fortitude they had in controlling that emotion under frightening circumstances is probably proportionate to the degree in which the emotion of fear has adversely affected them in later life.

What is hard to ascertain is to what degree the traumas of war affect a person. Combat veterans were affected the most but others also suffer from traumatic experiences. Some people are affected more than others are and it is not necessarily in direct proportion to the degree or frequency of their experiences. The human mind is only capable of experiencing a certain amount and degree of horrors before it is affected. What that amount and degree are depends upon the person and how it affects that mind can differ greatly among people.

I have seen buddies killed and wounded, seen blood and body parts, killed people, seen dead soldiers both friendly and enemy, seen dead kids, been in fearful situations, yet I am not sure how much it has affected me. I do not have nightmares or nervousness or guilt and do not have any apparent emotional problems because of these experiences. I can vividly recall traumatic experiences but before writing this book I rarely called them to mind. Since writing this book I have felt its effects but more from the cumulative effects of the war although there may be particular traumatic experiences that affected me. I have talked about the war more in the last year than the other twenty odd years combined, which is directly related to the writing of this book and in a sense the reliving of the war. Doing this has not been a good experience. They say that you're better off letting sleeping dogs lie but I did not. The "I do not give a damn" attitude came back, which led to abusing alcohol and some people while drinking. I realized this and stopped writing for a couple of months but I felt a compelling need to finish. The abuses started again. Now that I have nearly finished, hopefully my attitude will return to normal and the abuses will subside. There were also some personal difficulties in my present life that were part of the problem.

As far as the traumatic experiences are concerned I do not think I realized their affects until I wrote this book but now I realize it has affected me in more ways than I have ever thought.

A recent effect is the feeling I get since the Persian Gulf War, listening to all those non-veterans talk about war. It is upsetting to listen to the glorification of war by people who are probably as full of shit as some of the anti-war demonstrators were during the Vietnam era. Tomorrow is the big ticker tape parade in New York. I am debating whether or not to go. My heart goes out to the veterans who served, my old unit was there but I find it hard to deal with some of the phoniness. I will address that in the epilogue.

Some veterans were deeply affected by their traumatic experiences. They have nightmares, flashbacks, nervousness, and guilt. It just basically upsets their emotional stability. Why some and not others I do not know. What one experiences and how it affects him is a very individual reality.

One night, a few years after I was home, a bunch of us were in the bar, some of us started to leave, one of the guys walked into the avenue and was hit by a speeding car that was trying to elude a police chase. He was knocked fifteen to twenty feet in the air and landed across the street about twenty yards down the avenue. He was dead before he landed. This affected all of us differently. I was talking to a couple of them recently. One guy was so deeply affected that for about a year he just could not get it out of his mind. Another guy who was in the bar at the time, who came out and saw his friend dead, told me it had a profound effect on him and became a little emotional when we talked about it today. I can vividly picture the whole accident. I was the first one over there when he landed. I looked at him, he was dead, and I just walked away. It affected me for a couple of days but then I just took it in stride. Why we all had different emotional reactions to the same incident is probably because each individual must deal with his own emotions and then come to grips with the reality of the situation. It could lead people into their own reality because of the emotional impact of the situation.

In talking with these guys we all remembered the incident but we each had a little different perspective on what actually happened. Did our emotional involvement alter our reality from what actually took place? On comparing our recollections we all saw the incident a little bit differently whom, if any of us, remembered exactly what happened? In writing this book I can vividly recall each incident exactly the way I portrayed them but have emotional or traumatic experiences altered my recollections? I honestly do not believe so but the possibility exists.

When police are involved in a shooting they are usually treated for trauma. Some are effected greater than others. There was a fire a year or so ago where eighty-seven people were killed. Looking at the dead bodies some of the firefighters had to be hospitalized because of traumatic effect. Others were not as affected. The emotional effects of a traumatic experience on the human psyche is unique to that individual.

There is also a cumulative effect of traumatic experiences. I have a friend of mine who is a housing police officer. We were talking, he was on the job about eight years at the time. The effects of seeing people dead, or wounded, victims of other heinous crimes, day after day after day was bothering him. It was affecting his emotions. I tried to explain to him that what he was experiencing was actually a normal reaction. The human mind is not capable of accepting this type of long time exposure. There is only so much pain and suffering and horror that the human mind is capable of dealing with before it becomes affected. I drew parallels to Vietnam. He started to calm down and I suggested that he seek counseling.

Talking to a nurse who worked in the emergency room for over ten years, I could see the long-term effects that the traumatic experiences were having on her. There was an agreement that the mind was only capable of dealing with so much before there would have to be a negative effect on you.

My uncle was a Marine during WWII. He entered the service when he was seventeen and came home when he was twenty-one. He fought in the Pacific going from island to island. The cumulative and perhaps individual traumatic effects left him emotionally unstable. He could function but the effects of the war were apparent. He died on Christmas day while I was in Vietnam because of the effects of the war in which he fought.

Traumatic effects of combat have taken its toll on many soldiers in every war. The emotional instability that was created by the immediate shock of the horrors that one experienced or by taking of emotions to a different dimension can vary immensely. It ranges anywhere from people who were mildly bothered to that of people who became completely unstable. One guy from the neighborhood became so unstable that he was treated with electric shock therapy. I saw him the other day. He is functional, he recognizes me but the conversation barely gets past hello. He reminds me of a robot. It could break your heart.

Many Vietnam Veterans were affected greatly because of the individual and cumulative traumatic effects of their experiences during the war. This was exacerbated by the fact that there was no counseling, no therapy, nothing to help you with your potential problems. Unless you were immediately affected to the point that you could not deal with reality you were left on your own. Even some people who were immediately affected were not recognized and not treated. When veterans who had emotional problems returned, they were released into society to fend for themselves. This created havoc for the returning veterans, their families and society in general.

The government recognized the need to treat the police officer, the firefighter, but not the soldier. I cannot believe that they did not recognize the need for counseling for combat veterans. They recognized the need but would rather spend the money to fight the war than on the people who fought in it. Even the money that was allocated through Veterans hospitals was a sham. There was no real counseling. They created junkies out of veterans. They just pushed pills on them and hoped their problems would go away.

I do not know how many veterans or to what degree they were affected by their traumatic experiences but I do know that there were many veterans who were not given the opportunity to deal with their problems because of government's callousness, lack of concern, or just outright refusal to deal with the problems of the soldiers who fought for their country.

Trauma was not the only thing that affected your emotions. The parameters of your emotions were expanded because of the war, especially for a combat soldier. It is like being in love for the first time. The emotion was always there but once you had the experience it grew in dramatic proportions. Then when love was no longer there you were susceptible to many negative effects because of this experience. Hopefully you grew from this and were better prepared for the next time you fell in love but each time would take its toll.

The combat veteran would have emotions grow in dramatic proportions in such things as fear, hate, anger, loneliness, survival, compassion, insecurity and the effects of these emotions could exact a dramatic toll.

Once you were in love you know that you could never shrink the parameters back to the point that they were before you experienced it. When the negative aspects of lost love began to manifest themselves you became defensive, susceptible to rebound love, withdrawn or overwrought.

The combat veteran will also never be able to shrink the parameters back to the point they were before he experienced them. The negative affects of each emotion can become difficult to handle. The more emotions that you experienced and the frequency of these could exact a toll that in many instances just become overwhelming. Even if they did not become overwhelming they will have a lasting impact.

Take anger for example. I have shown reasons why a veteran could become angry at the government. Now if you take a veteran whose parameters for anger have been expanded he can become filled with that much more anger. It could get to the point where the anger could become out of control because of this capacity for anger. This could happen to any of the emotions. The likelihood of loss of control, because of this expanded capacity, will be much more prevalent in the veteran than it would be for the average person. The controlling of these emotions for the veteran will be a more difficult process than it would be for the average person but it is something that he must deal with in order to maintain a stable existence.

Also the emotions themselves might be different from what you might expect them to be. Take loneliness. You would expect that a veteran would miss home and their loved ones but combat can bring loneliness to a different dimension. At times you get a feeling that you are the only one there, you are isolated, by yourself. The feeling that it is only you can become chilling and fill you with an emptiness that is hard to describe. It is only a temporary feeling but leaves an immense emotional impact.

Most emotions can be taken to a different dimension during combat. I experienced a hate and anger that led to a rage in me that took me to a dimension that is beyond my capabilities of description but I will try to explain how it happens. Picture a graph with the numbers from one to ten. There are two horizontal lines. One fluctuating between eight and ten and the other between one and three. Within these lines contains your thoughts, your emotions, and your experiences, in essence your reality. Now you are confronted with an intense emotional experience that goes beyond the parameters of the graph, lets say to twenty. This sudden surge creates a vacuum that pulls the rest of your reality into this new dimension. Your being is now experiencing this new dimension which is a completely different reality from where you started. Rod Steiger would call this the twilight zone but it is a very real and different reality. Hopefully the gravity of your original reality will pull you back into that state.

Experiencing this dimension of your emotions has to psychologically effect you. For some there is an immediate effect because being in this state can become intolerable. The mind can create a subterfuge because of the intolerability of this state of being. This is probably what causes what is commonly referred to as shell-shocked. It might cause a loss in memory or just keep all or part of you in that new reality. Even if your experience does not take you to the point where you have an immediate negative reaction there has to be a long-term effect caused by this emotional experience.

Experiencing of emotions in a heightened state, especially when it evolves into a different dimension is probably what causes the phenomenon that is known as flashbacks. When you get back home and you become involved in a highly emotional state of being the comparison that your mind makes is your experience during combat. So there becomes transference to the emotion that you experienced during combat, recreating the experience, which we call flashbacks. There are also other elements that may trigger flashback. One time the smell of gunpowder immediately brought me back to a situation that I faced in Vietnam.

Flashbacks occur because your mind relates a current experience to one in which you had previously. Vietnam being the most intense experience that your mind has dealt with, it becomes understandable that a current emotional state would reflect back to the point of its highest emotional comparison.

There is something called delayed stress syndrome that I really do not know that much about but have probably been affected by during the writing of this book. The stress and emotions that you encountered during Vietnam are probably the most intense that you will encounter during your life. As time goes on, the intensity of the emotions that you experience during the war can just overlap your current emotional situation. This could happen five, ten, twenty or more years down the road. They once again become an upsetting factor that you must now deal with again or for perhaps the first time. What causes them to overlap at this time might be some type of emotional flashback or perhaps suppressed emotions that are just working their way to the surface. I do not know, but it is a real phenomenon.

None of what I have described about emotions, trauma or anything else is textbook they are merely my perceptions and evaluations of those perceptions.

The perception that people have toward Vietnam Veterans may not coincide with reality. I have had more than one person say to me that I am the only Vietnam Veteran that they know not to be affected by the war. That most veterans just seem to be a bunch of wackos. I usually do not entertain such discussions because it just becomes too complex of a discussion for that person to draw a legitimate understanding. This is one of the reasons why I am writing this book. People's perceptions can be off because of their lack of understanding of the experience and the problems that it caused. For them to think that I was not affected is just as naive as to think that most veterans have been affected to the point that they are out of control. All Vietnam Veterans have been affected but considering the circumstances the majority have adjusted reasonably well. These are the ones who have not become highly visible. The high visibility of certain veterans gives the impression that most veterans are maladjusted.

People's perceptions can become further deluded by a consensus that blames Vietnam for problems that it might not have caused. There are three guys who walk Flatbush Ave., all apparently deranged, who are perceived by the people as being that way because they were in Vietnam. I know all three. One guy was never in the service. Another was in the army but suffered head injuries during basic training which left him that way. The third is a Vietnam Vet. We were in some classes together at Brooklyn College. We both graduated and he went on for his Masters. He was a highly emotional person who lost part of his foot in Vietnam. Over the years he hit the skids. He became homeless and was living on the bowery for years. He came back to the neighborhood and his mental capacities were greatly diminished. I would give him odd jobs now and then. We were talking one day and I could not help to wonder how he got so screwed up. I thought it was because of Vietnam and was I asking him about it. To my surprise he thought he lost control because of the fact the he was an abused child. Not sexually but physically and emotionally because of an extremely authoritative father, that Vietnam was probably the catalyst that caused the negative affects from a previous psychological problem.

People's perception about the Vietnam Veteran is very negative, so when they see a negative situation it is easy to blame it on the effects of the war, when in fact, the war might not be the root cause of the problem.

The perception that the veteran had upon his return about what he was to expect was his initial awakening as to what was to come. Many veterans expected things to be the same as when they had left. They very much wanted things to be the same, thereby deluding themselves into believing that in spite of their experiences, that they were basically the same. Neither was true. Change is inevitable.

The drastic changes that took place both to society and to the veteran soon became apparent. That gave a little bit of a jolt to the veteran who was now on his road to readjustment. When he subsequently encountered the potential problems that we have discussed he started out at a disadvantage. The jolt that he encountered when he realized that change had taken place to both him and his present environment left him a little bit off keel. Then all the other factors came into play, which became more difficult to deal with because he was not addressing them with both feet on the ground.

Most Vietnam Veterans were between nineteen and twenty-two years old when they returned home. This is a difficult age for anyone, no less someone who had just experienced a war. Then he had to deal with the initial reaction to change, possible traumatic and emotional problems, acceptance, attitude, moral dilemmas, the excitement factor, drugs, alcohol, recognition, relationships and all the other factors that he had to contend with in order to facilitate his readjustment back into society. Many veterans could not deal with one or more variables, thereby never fully readjusting.

There were veterans that not only had to contend with any or all of these factors, they also had their own physical disabilities to deal with, which compounded their readjustment. They might be blind, deaf, speechless, lost all or part of their limbs or vital organs. They had to adjust to their physical disabilities and any emotional or psychological scars that they might have. Plus everything else, there were some who would spend the rest of their lives in Veterans Hospitals.

There was a perception by the people in general that looked upon the Vietnam veteran in a very misinformed way. They wondered why the Vietnam veteran seemed to have so many problems when the veterans from other wars did not seem to be that affected. What happened in Vietnam that was different or was there something lacking in the Vietnam veteran.

Although every war is different the combat veteran from Vietnam probably experienced the same fears, emotions and traumatic effects as any combat soldier in any war. After W.W.II and Korea there were numerous combat veterans who were emotional affected because of their experiences during the war. The effects of their combat experiences affected them emotionally probably to the same proportion as the Vietnam combat veteran was affected. The difference between them and us was not our combat experiences. All combat veterans to one degree or another were affected by their individual horrors that they might have experienced. From my own empirical evidence I saw a high rate of alcoholism and emotional problems in combat veterans of both Korea and W.W.II but it just did not seem to draw the attention of the public. There are numerous reasons for this. One reason is the number of soldiers that actually served in combat. If it was twenty percent, it was probably closer to fifteen percent, out of that twenty percent let us say that fifty percent of them were affected to a noticeable degree because of their combat experience. This would leave nine out of ten veterans with no noticeable effects because of their service during these wars. If they did not experience readjustment problems back into society then the overwhelming majority of veterans seemed to be stable, without any apparent effects from the war. The veterans that were affected were a very small percentage. Easy for them to go unnoticed, especially at a time when the media, television in particular, did not command the audiences nor focus on the problem Veterans, but they did exist.

For the Vietnam Veteran it was different. Percentage wise you probably had the same twenty percent or less that were combat veterans. By combat veterans I mean those that were actually physically engaged in fighting the enemy. The difference between Vietnam and most other wars was that there were no front lines. So even though you might not be physically engaging the enemy you were psychologically affected by fear and the reality that you were in a combat zone no matter what your MOS, job, was in Vietnam. This greatly raised the percentage of people who were psychologically and emotionally affected by combat even though they might not have actually been engaging the enemy in combat.

Then these veterans were brought back to the world and faced the myriad of readjustment problems, which was not the case for the Korean and especially the W.W.II veterans, their readjustment problems, coupled with the extremely high exposure by most Vietnam veterans to the psychological stress of constantly being in a war zone, is what created the proportionally higher number of veterans that were affected by their wartime service.

The media focused its attention for over a decade on the war, the anti-war movement, and the problem veterans. This was a constant reminder to the Vietnam veteran and created problems in and of itself. The animal that we call the Vietnam veteran is a unique entity and in many ways different from veterans of others wars.

There were many complexities that faced the Vietnam veteran and a society that was not ready to face these complexities. The longer society ignored the problems, the more these problems seemed to affect society. It reached the point where society because of its inaction did not know how to deal with the situation. So in essence they closed their eyes and hoped we would go away. We did not go away. We were left to deal with our problems without the necessary help that should have been in place for us. For better or worse the Vietnam Veteran will leave his mark on society just as society has left its mark on the veteran. We will both be dealing with our problems for many years to come.

As far as I am concerned, my readjustment was a little smoother than most although I faced some bumpy roads and still have a hurdle or two left to negotiate. I thank my family for being an integral part in my readjustment.

When I was separated from the service I faced the immediate choice of whether or not to accept an appointment to the NYC Fire Department. I had taken the test and was called for the job while I was serving in Vietnam. There was a ninety-day period in which I had to accept. The fire department was an attractive job and I had family in the department but it was not the right time for me. The discipline that would have been required was something that I was not ready to deal with. Besides I had my mind made up to finish college. I briefly went to St. Francis College before the service but that was a disaster. I was going to return there but because of financial considerations Brooklyn College became my choice. It turned out for the better. Brooklyn College was an excellent school that had a diverse faculty and curriculum that allowed me to work out many moral questions that I was pondering. I found it a little anti-social, whether it was I or the school is debatable but I did not need social interaction from the school. That was attained through friends and family.

Love entered my life soon after returning. She was a beautiful woman in all aspects and helped me immensely. The relationship lasted over six years. She saw something in me that I was not totally aware of, the excitement factor. There was something in me that needed to get out. That needed to be satiated and unfortunately it caused us to break up.

During this time I went into business with my cousin. It was a bar, rock club. Many stories both good and bad could be told but basically this gave me both a freedom and a discipline. The negative aspect was it helped foster the "I don't care what happenes." Marijuana was also a big influence during this period. The venture lasted about three years and it was some experience.

Then I went back to school to finish eight credits that were needed for a degree. With degree in hand I went out seeking a teaching position. It was the mid-seventies, NYC was in a financial crisis and teaching positions were hard to find. Fortunately through friends, I wound up with a position in the NYC high school system. I liked teaching and became very good at it. They bounced me around from school to school because of the financial crisis but that did not bother me I liked the experience; besides, many teachers were being laid off and I was working. The last school that I worked in I had taught in previously and when a position opened they requested that I return. It was a nice school to teach in because the faculty was supportive and the student body was challenging.

It was the last day of a regular class session and the security guards pulled their annual sick out. The faculty was very sensitive to the fact that there were few security guards in the school. I had a free period but they assigned me to cafeteria duty. The school had a policy where only seniors were allowed outside during lunch. The rest of the student body was required remain in the cafeteria. I was in the middle of the cafeteria when I spotted a commotion by one of the exits. There was a group of about fifteen black students trying to go outside. There was a science teacher about five feet six who was stopping them from going outside. I was walking toward the area when one of the students threw a punch, hitting the teacher. He picked up a chair to defend himself. A couple of more students started throwing punches. I rushed over, grabbed one kid who was still throwing punches, held him with one arm and with my free hand pulled another kid off of the teacher. By this time another teacher had come to our aid and we managed to corral six of the students. We brought them into the principal's office and turned them over to an assistant principal. The bell rang and I had to go to my next class. The following period I was on my lunch break. I went to the principal's office to see what was happening. There was no one in the outer office. I requested to talk to the principal but they told me he was "in conference". I tracked down the A.P. to whom we turned the students over and asked him what had happened. He told me that he went into the other office and the students ran away.

"What do you mean they ran away? You know who they are. Go find them."

He started giving me a song and a dance about it being the last day of school and whatever.

"Are you trying to tell me that you are going to let these kids go? That there is nothing you are going to do about it? These kids assaulted a teacher and would have hurt him badly if I did not intercede. Find those kids and if you will not do anything then I want them arrested."

He kept mumbling about nothing. I felt my adrenaline pumping. I left and went to the teacher's cafeteria. I saw an assistant principal with whom I was friendly and started to explain the situation. He knew about it and basically was giving me the same routine that the other A.P. was spouting. I told him that this was bullshit. "A teacher was assaulted. Another teacher and myself put ourselves on the line and you are just going to let these kids get away with it. I cannot accept that. Either do something or give me the names of the students and I will have them arrested." Not that I was necessarily looking to have them arrested but they had to be dealt with in an appropriate manner. The discussion continued but got nowhere. The bell rang so I went to my next class. During the eighth period they sent me a note to go to the A.P. office after the period. When I arrived, there was just myself and the one A.P. He was still trying to explain to me why nothing was going to be done and that they really were not sure who these students were. I told him that he knew who they were and if he did not that I would point them out to him. Besides, the other teacher knew at least three of them by name. Finally I asked what was going on. Were they afraid to do something because these students were black? He told me not to bring race into it. I was not looking to put race into it but what else are you leading me to believe? If these were Italian, Irish, or Jewish kids you would have their parents down here so fast that my head would spin. They would at least be on suspension and probably expelled from the school. I asked if he thought he was doing them a favor by doing nothing. "You are hurting these kids. They're out there right now on the streets bragging how they beat up a teacher. What happens when they come back for exams or next year? Do you think you are going to able to control them or you just do not care because they are black? Are you just afraid of the blacks?" He told me to leave race out of it but he had nothing else to say. I asked for the names again but he would not give them to me. Instead he handed me a U.F.T. pamphlet on security. I told him that I put my life on the line to protect a fellow teacher and if this administration did not see fit to back me, then I did not know what I was doing in this school. He had nothing to say so I left his office and went home.

I read the pamphlet and somewhere it stated something to the effect that if a teacher is attacked that they should do nothing because the immediate reprisals that they faced could be much worse than the original attack. I could not believe it, and our own union put out this pamphlet. I knew right there that I had to stop teaching. In the past I had physically broken up fights between students, stepped in between a gangs of Blacks and Puerto Ricans about to go at it, defusing the situation, and sooner or later another situation would arise and I again would put my life on the line. This would not bother me. The fact that I would put my life on the line and the administration would not back me I could not tolerate. I had been in that position in Vietnam and would not do so again. My teaching days ended shortly thereafter.

Just to clarify a point. Race was not the issue with me. This was a predominately white school but the others in which I taught were predominately Black or Hispanic. I communicated well with the student body and found the diversity in cultures enriching. I just could not fathom even the most liberal of philosophies justifying letting these students go. It hurt the student, the faculty, and the school. I honestly believe at the time that they were afraid of the Black students or perhaps the repercussions from their community, although they would never admit to it and maybe did not actually realize it.

Whatever their reasoning was, it became clear to me that the politics of the situation had evolved to a point where my interests were not being protected. If I was not in Vietnam perhaps my actions would have been different but to remain teaching in a system that left me with a feeling of abandonment was just too much for me to accept at the time.

Even though I enjoyed most aspects of teaching my passions lay more toward business and politics. Shortly after leaving teaching I decided to run for political office. I did not have the backing of the regular political organization and lost the election but I did much better than anyone expected. This opened up a new world and I became very involved in various community organizations.

My basic feelings were that the community was changing, crime was on the rise, the neighborhood was starting to deteriorate and somebody had to do something. That somebody could not be someone else. I was the veteran who fought the war and now it was my time to fight to preserve the community. The fight took me from being president of a neighborhood civic association, director and eventually president of a local development corporation. Later I became chairman of a coalition for tuition tax credits, was involved in environmental campaigns, helped develop an alternative high school program, and spent a lot of time trying to stop the increase of drugs and ridding the community of drug dens.

The one thing that I did not get deeply involved in was Veterans' issues. That was basically because of my perceptions of the people involved. They seemed to be holding onto the war, not letting themselves break away or be weaned off of it. They seemed to cultivate an attitude that was negative, they were blaming the war and the government for the shortcomings of the veterans. While there might have been a lot of credence in what they were saying, this was not for me. I wanted a positive attitude, to leave the war behind me and get on with the rest of my life, to stop blaming the world and find a positive avenue of approach in the direction that I was taking. This left me with some guilt because I should have been more involved with Veterans' issues but it just was not good for my development at the time.

Then came a very traumatic moment for me. My father passed away. It affected me deeply although I did not have problems adjusting to it. My father was an officer who was decorated for heroism during W.W.II. He was very patriotic to the point of "My country right or wrong," yet made me aware of some ill affects of his service. He felt proud to serve in the army yet felt that the army had robbed him of four years of his life. When he was discharged he became a state trooper, then a customs inspector, and to his regret, the owner of a local tavern. I am sure that feeling runs through many veterans that their lives would be different if they were not in the service, the Vietnam veteran in particular. Most of us were not in the service for four years but the problem of readjustment might have taken more years away from us than that.

The next six years of my life were spent in the restaurant business, doing community work and for two years as an elected Democratic Party Official, State Committee-District Leader. The restaurant was a seven day a week operation that I owned for six years. Between the restaurant, community work, politics, and falling in love again, it left little time for anything else. Alcohol was barely part of my life and there were no other measurable effects from Vietnam. At least not that I realized.

Being elected to elective office was an interesting and eye opening experience. I was elected because they needed a visible Irishman to balance a Jewish and Black ticket. I fit the bill. To get into a discussion on politics would take too long but there is one thing that I did realize. Politicians have one basic goal. That is to get elected. If they can get elected by helping the community, great. If they can get elected by hurting the community, so be it.

The one thing that politics did allow me to do was get a little bit involved with Veterans' issues. I had the opportunity to question presidential candidates on their views concerning veterans' benefits and in particular their feelings towards the P.O.W.-M.I.A. issue. Not that it accomplished that much but it made them aware that we would not let this issue die. I became heavily involved in Senator Al Gore's race for president, not only because he was a Vietnam Veteran but he was the best candidate for the job. Politically in a district that was sixty five percent Black, in a race that Jesse Jackson was involved, this was not a wise decision but I had to go with my convictions.

On the positive side I became involved with a living memorial where we are working on having a park in order to plant a tree for every soldier who was killed or missing in action from Brooklyn. Congressman Charles Schumer has been working hard with us on this endeavor. Do not mistake this for any type of political quid pro quo because it is not. I know Congressman Schumer for years but he did not endorse me when I ran for office. I just feel this story is pertinent. Congressman Schumer is a friend of the Vietnam veteran. I was talking to him one day when he asked if I had ever been to the Vietnam Memorial in Washington. I told him I had not. He said, "I know this might sound a little morbid but when I need to think to work out a solution for a problem that I might be facing in Congress, I go to the Memorial. There is a peace there that gives me strength to help me make a decision. Does that sound strange?" I did not know what to say. Congressman Schumer is not a Vietnam Veteran but he has our interests at heart.

My elected political career lasted only two years, losing the next election by less than ninety votes but I kept my hand in the arena.

My last relationship lasted for over seven years. We lived together for most of that time and she was a bright and caring woman. They were good times for both of us at least until the last year. She was looking for a little more stability than I had to offer. I was not affected by the excitement factor. That had been more or less satisfied but I was not ready for a mundane type of existence. The nine to five world just was not appealing to me. How much this was an effect of the war I was not really sure.

The break up affected me adversely but also gave me time to reflect on where I was in life. That had both good and bad effects.

I decided to look for another business venture but, I also wanted to write this book. My former girlfriend used to encourage me to do so. I also had a need to try to relate the experience to a growing population who did not seem to understand. I took a job as a bartender to pay the bills while writing this book. During this time is when the Vietnam War had its greatest negative effect on me. Perhaps it was delayed stress syndrome or the fact that I was reliving the war in my mind but whatever it was, it was not good. The abuse of alcohol, enhanced by the fact that I was tending bar, was becoming too frequent an ally of the "I do not care attitude." I was starting to get a little pessimistic for the first time in my life.

I was never as bitter as some veterans were about the war. I know that it was ill- conceived, ill-planned, caused the needless loss of the life and limb to thousands upon thousands of Americans and the post-war effects were horrendous. It will probably be viewed as one of the greatest tragedies in our history yet this was part, as tragic as it was, of an overall plan of foreign policy to stop Soviet expansion. As strange as this might sound when the Berlin

Wall came tumbling down I took pride in the fact that in a small way my involvement in Vietnam helped foster this. However, I am sure this is a minority view among Vietnam Veterans.

There are many variables that affected the Vietnam veteran and some of them could leave him very bitter. What depressed many veterans was lack of recognition or understanding of his experience. He watched many non-veterans lead seemingly normal lives but he knew his life had been changed yet nobody seemed to care. He was an unfortunate product of history that nobody wanted to deal with. A pat on the back and recognition of the Veterans' sacrifice for society would have gone a long way in combating this bitterness and depression.

What really is depressing me is the state of affairs here in America. In theory you fight a war to preserve freedom and tranquility at home. We no longer have this. This is going to sound chauvinistic and I realize that this book is not written gender neutral, but where have we as men evolved to when it is no longer safe for our women to walk the streets? Our mothers, daughters, wives, sisters, children, seniors and even ourselves face the prospect where is not safe for us to live in the cities in America. This way of life is spreading to the suburbs we fought wars to preserve our domestic peace and now it seems to be eroding around us.

I worked hard over the years to try to maintain a stable community but it appears to be a losing battle. My sister called me recently to ask my opinion about moving to a house in the Belle Harbor section of New York City. It was only a few miles away and she did not want to leave Brooklyn but it was a safer area. I never thought I would say this but I told her to move. Our family has been in Brooklyn for over one hundred years but she and her husband have two children to consider. Crime in the area is up and drugs are taking their toll. Her area was still good but the surrounding areas were starting to have a deteriorating effect on the stability of the community. I know that running away will not solve these problems but I am no longer certain that without a drastic social change that these problems are solvable. Do you stay and fight or do you look out for the immediate welfare of your family?

The way of life that we have known no longer exists. I cannot help but feel that as men we have failed to protect our family and the community. The fact that the women's movement has made them equal partners in this failure does not reconcile the fact that we have evolved as men and women to create a society that no longer assures peace and tranquility.

This has dwelled in my mind and has affected my outlook in many areas. I become a little bit depressed when I realize that the place that I call home will eventually not be there for me. Not that I do not want to stay and fight, because if things continue in their present direction that will be your only alternative no matter where you go, but with the present battle plans I do not see a way of winning. The changes that must take place are too radical for the present social climate and would be unacceptable to the powers that be. If I get married and raise a family I would probably seek out an area that would afford safety and tranquility, as temporary as that might be.

With all this on my mind, linked with the effects that I have experienced while writing this book, the fact that the women I loved have left me, my business prospects are dubious at best, my money is near depleted and I do not know what direction I am headed, points to a future that is not painting a bright picture. All this translates to a very low point in my life. Any time I feel low I look back at Vietnam. Not as some other veterans might, using the experience as an excuse or a crutch for their present difficulties, although in many cases it is understandable. I look at Vietnam as the worst possible experience that could ever happen to me and if I could survive that I could survive anything. It gives me a strength and the more I draw on that strength I realize that I can overcome any difficulties that might come my way. I will survive.

Epilogue: Desert Storm

I have heard it said that Operation Desert Storm was in essence the last battle of the Vietnam War. I do not agree with that but I can see where one might draw comparisons.

This segment is being written for the soldiers who have served in that war but before I get to that there are comments that I must make on the war itself.

The immediacy and intensity of patriotism that swamped the country was somewhat surprising. The basic attitude that I heard since Vietnam was that I would not let my children fight in a war after what happened in Vietnam. Now there was this surge of patriotism. Why?

The nature of the war itself was more defined. There was a villain in Sadam Hussain that allowed the American people to be able to focus on the enemy. The losing of the Vietnam War never sat well on the American psyche. Now we had a new enemy, seemingly moral justification, and a war that was inevitably going to be won by our nation and its allies. That made the American people feel good because they could again perceive themselves as the most powerful nation on earth.

Americans went all out in their support for the troops, in part because collectively as a nation we felt guilty about the lack of support that we gave our troops who served in Vietnam. It helped clear our conscience. We also did not want to make the same mistake again.

This new-found patriotism should have been welcome by me but instead it became somewhat perplexing. It was nice to see America united, but again I started to question the integrity of some of the people involved. The college students who were the backbone of the anti-war movement during the Vietnam era were now the backbone of the pro-war movement. I started to come to the conclusion that it was because it did not affect them. There was a team in the Big East Basketball Conference that had a player from Spain or Italy on its squad. Every player in the conference, and probably the country, wore an American flag on their uniform. This player declined to do so. He felt that it would be unpatriotic to his country for him to wear the flag of another nation. The college students booed him off the court. He left the school and went back to his country.

These students did this in the name of patriotism. If they were so patriotic, why didn't they go and join the service? They were "Rah rah America" but few, if any, left the confines of their classrooms to go and serve their country. With this surge of patriotism the military should have had a surge of enlistments. They did not. It is easy to be pro-war if you know that you personally do not have to be part of it. If they reenacted the draft I wonder what the attitude on the college campuses would have been. For that matter, the attitude of the country in general. If the sons or perhaps daughters of Americans became eligible to be drafted, do you think this surge of patriotism would have existed? It is nice to have someone else fight your wars for you.

Today's college students with their aura of false patriotism remind me in a sense of the college students of the seventies whose anti-war demonstrations dissipated as soon as they ended the draft.

It is understandable why the people and military would both rather not have a draft but is this the right policy? War is the ultimate commitment and sacrifice by a nation and its people to defend the policies of that nation. If the fighting of that war is being done by a segment of the population rather than participation by everyone in that nation the commitment that might be made and the policies that might be defended might not reflect the will of the people. It could lead a nation down the wrong path.

If someone else is fighting the war the commitments and sacrifices do not become a reality to you. They do not hit home. It becomes natural that good PR could sway your perceptions because you were not called on to make a commitment or sacrifice. Grenada, Panama, and Desert Storm were all made more palatable because we personally did not have to focus on our individual commitment and sacrifice. I personally agree with the commitments that were made in these instances but I am also aware that the present policy of an all-volunteer army can alter our perceptions and possibly lead us in a dangerous direction.

As far as wars go, Desert Storm was a masterpiece. It was planned and executed with the utmost proficiency. Every effort was made to insure that there was no needless loss of American lives. The political military intelligence was kept at bay at least until the end. I thought it should have lasted a few more days in order to overthrow Sadam Hussain but perhaps the geo-political strategy was best served by having Sadam Hussain militarily crippled yet still in control.

The main problem that I see, and I do not like to call it a problem, is that it was accomplished so easily. This could lead the government and the people, who lack the necessity for commitment and sacrifice, to think that other wars will be accomplished in this manner. Hopefully there will be no other wars but if a situation arises where the airpowers becomes restricted because of the indeterminable boundaries or geographical obstacles, once again many American lives could be lost. Do not let Desert Storm be a banner for pro-war.

The Desert Storm Veteran will not have many obstacles in their readjustment back into society but that does not mean there will be none. The military gave counseling about what to expect when they return. This will be extremely helpful but there will still be adjustments. Many veterans were older with families and the fact that their spouses acted independently, perhaps for the first time, will create a need for adjustments by both parties especially when decisions occur that might have been previously made basically by one party.

The overwhelming acceptance that the veterans enjoyed upon their return might change as time goes on. When the Desert Storm Veterans join the traditional Veterans' organizations they will initially be welcomed with open arms but because of the brevity of their war it is inevitable that they will be confronted by the veterans of all the other wars with the "I fought in the real war syndrome." This is going to affect the Desert Storm Veteran because for the great majority it will have a ring of truth to it when they ponder the realities. For those who were actually in combat this is going to be very frustrating, because combat is combat. For veterans that were never near combat it could cause feelings of inadequacy. You could start doubting yourself and perhaps feel deep down that you were not as real a soldier as those from other wars. Do not let this happen. The fact that the magnitude of your war was less than other wars had nothing to do with your commitment. You were put into a war zone. You were willing to face anything that came your way. You served your country honorably. So because of these factors you're as much a veteran as anyone who served in any war. Granted, you did not face what other veterans faced and you should respect them for what they went through, but you were willing to do anything that had to be done. That puts you on an equal plane.

There will be veterans who will become bitter because their lives were disrupted or their jobs were not waiting for them or they were the forgotten soldiers who were left there long after the war ended. The only thing I can say to you is do not let the bitterness get to you. Bite the bullet and get on with the rest of your life.

Fear is the element that will cause the most problems for the Desert Storm veterans. Remember, there is nothing wrong with fear. It is your reaction to fear that makes you or breaks you. The problem for most Desert Storm veterans is that they never got to know their reaction in combat situation. You were sent into a war zone, that is an automatic cause for fear. You faced the possibility of chemical warfare, that was cause for increased fear but there was no reaction that allowed you to vent or know your reaction to your fear, at least for the majority who were not involved in combat situations. The fear that you were experiencing was real and probably had the opportunity to grow on you where it could reach a level that might have become out of proportion with the actual reality that you faced. You might have wondered, if you were this scared now, what is going to happen if you were actually in combat? You will never know but do not let it bother you. We all at one time or another were that scared and probably more so. Most of us when it came to combat dealt with it in a proper manner. The odds are that you also would have dealt with it in a proper manner. This does not mean that the fear that you experienced will not affect you. It has to. Your parameters for fear were somewhat expanded, thereby expanding that emotion for you. Even though you were scared, if you did not let that fear cause you to be out of control at the time, you should not let the reccollection of how scared you were affect you adversely now. Both situations are normal for your experience.

For veterans who experienced combat there is no need for me to explain fear to you. Either you dealt with it or you did not.

There probably was not enough time for the cumulative effects of traumatic experiences to effect you, but the immediate affects of traumatic experiences could strike anyone. If you find something bothering you, immediately get counseling. Fear can also be a traumatic experience so if you feel it adversely affecting you, get counseling.

Another problem that I perceived for the Desert Storm veteran could be a delay in the realization of the effects of the war. The overwhelming support and acceptance that you receive might momentarily overshadow some existing problems. If you experience problems in the future do not try to overlook them. Deal with them. You were put into a war zone and that has to in one way or another change you from the person you were before you went there. Try to realize this change and adjust your life accordingly.

To all Desert Storm Veterans, thank you and good luck with your adjustment.

To the people who think that because of your support for the Desert Storm troops somehow made amends for Vietnam. It did not.

To the people who think that Desert Storm was somehow the last battle of the Vietnam War. It was not. The last battle of the Vietnam War will not be won until all of the POW/MIAs return home.

To the people who want to do something for the Vietnam Veterans. Put pressure on the government to change their policies in order to account for and bring home the remaining POW/MIA's.

Thank you.

CPSIA information can be obtained at www.ICGtesting.com
Printed in the USA
BVOW02*0806170813

328578BV00003B/62/A